AMERICAN ORIENTAL SERIES
VOLUME 34

THE NARRATIVE OF BHOJA (BHOJAPRABANDHA)

BY BALLĀLA OF BENARES

AMERICAN ORIENTAL SERIES

VOLUME 34

AMERICAN ORIENTAL SOCIETY
NEW HAVEN, CONNECTICUT
1950

THE NARRATIVE OF BHOJA
(BHOJAPRABANDHA)

BY

BALLĀLA OF BENARES

TRANSLATED FROM SANSKRIT

BY

LOUIS H. GRAY

AMERICAN ORIENTAL SOCIETY
NEW HAVEN, CONNECTICUT
1950

MADE IN UNITED STATES OF AMERICA

J. H. FURST COMPANY, BALTIMORE, MARYLAND

To

MARY

Loyal Friend

of

Many Years

To

MARY

Loving Friend

and

Many Years

CONTENTS

INTRODUCTION

Nothing seems to be known concerning Ballāla (or Ballāladeva Daivajña or Ballālamiśra) of Benares except that he was the son of Trimalla, son of Rāma, son of Cintāmaṇi; father of Rāma, Kṛṣṇa Gaṇaka or Kṛṣṇa Daivajña (a commentator on astronomy in the reign of Jahāngīr, 1605-1627), Govinda (who composed a commentary on the famous astronomical treatise *Sūryasiddhānta* in 1603), Mahādeva, and Raṅganātha (the author of the *Gūḍārthaprakāśika* in 1604, also a commentary on the *Sūryasiddhānta*); and grandfather of Viśvarūpa Gaṇaka Munīśvara (a commentator on astronomical works and the author of the astronomical *Siddhāntasārvabhauma* in 1651; Aufrecht, i, 118[a]; 166[b]; 488[a]; 586[a]; 722[a]; ii, 138[b]). He flourished, therefore, toward the end of the sixteenth and the beginning of the seventeenth century (Aufrecht, i, 368[a]; ii, 83[a]; and *Catalogus Codicum Sanscriticorum Bibliothecae Bodleianae,* Oxford, 1864, pp. 150-151).

The only work ascribed to Ballāla is the *Bhojaprabandha*, or 'Narrative of Bhoja.' This Bhoja (also called Bhojarāja, Bhojanarendra, and Bhojanṛpati), King of Dhārā in Mālava (the modern Dhār in Mālwa, Central Provinces), was the son and successor of Sindhurāja (the Sindhula of the *Bhojaprabandha, -la* being a late hypocoristic termination in substitution for the august *-rāja*; cf. A. Hilka, *Die altindischen Personennamen,* Breslau, 1910, pp. 24, 69, 99), who ascended the throne about 995 and reigned until about 1010 (Duff, pp. 102, 109, 300; G. Bühler, *Epigraphia Indica,* i [1892], 228-229). Bhoja's own reign lasted until about 1055, when he was succeeded by Jayasiṁha (Duff, pp. 124, 300). According to the *Bhojaprabandha* (*6*), simply copied from Merutuṅga's *Prabandhacintāmaṇi* (Mer. 57; Taw. 32), completed in 1306 (Winternitz, ii, 332; Krishnamachariar, p. 207), a Brāhman prophesied that Bhoja should reign for 'fifty years and five, seven months, and three days,' whereas he actually ruled only forty-five. Supposing, as a most improbable hypothesis, that the slightest importance should be attached to this vaticination, *pañcāśat-* 'fifty' may have been substituted for *catvāriṁśat-* 'forty' merely to meet the exigencies of the metre and further to glorify Bhoja.

On the other hand, Muñja (Vākpati II), represented in the *Bhojaprabandha* as the younger brother of Sindhula (Sindhurāja), was really his elder brother and his predecessor as King; and instead of renouncing the throne in remorse at his attempted murder of Bhoja and retiring to a life of penance, as in Ballāla's romantic tale, he enjoyed a fairly long reign from 974 until about 995, when, after many military vicissitudes, he was conquered in battle and executed by the Chālukya Tailapa II (Duff, pp. 97, 102, 300; Bühler, pp. 226-228). The true order of succession, then, was Muñja, Sindhula, and Bhoja (974-*c.* 995; *c.* 995-*c.* 1010; *c.* 1010-*c.* 1055), instead of Ballāla's sequence of Sindhula, Muñja, and Bhoja.

Into further historical details of Bhoja's career (Lassen, iii, 836-885; Rājendralāla Mitra, 'Bhoja Rájá of Dhárá and his Homonyms,' *Journal of the Royal Asiatic Society of Bengal,* 1863, pp. 91-110; Bühler, pp. 229-233), which have no connexion with the *Bhojaprabandha,* it is scarcely necessary to enter here; and this is equally true of several inscriptions of Northern India which mention Bhoja's name (listed, with references, by F. Kielhorn, *A List of the Inscriptions of Northern India from about A. D. 400,* Calcutta, 1899 = *Appendix to Epigraphia Indica,* v, nos. 57, 67, 79, 82[?], 195, 430; also his *List of Inscriptions of Southern India,* etc., Calcutta, 1902 = *Appendix to Epigraphia Indica,* vi, no. 152). Suffice it to say that he waged several wars, some successful, others not, and that the circumstances and even the date of his death are quite uncertain (cf. Duff, p. 109; Taw. pp. ix-xi). It is, however, very possible that, as Merutuṅga says (Taw. 74-75), Bhoja died soon after defeat by Karṇadeva of Chedi (1042-1122) in alliance with the Chaulukya Bhīmadeva I (1022-1063; Duff, p. 112).

Ballāla, who terminates his work abruptly, says nothing about the end of his hero's life, possibly because Bhoja was forced to flee when Dhārā was stormed by Someśvara I (1040-1069); and our author—here in conformity with the conventions of the Sanskrit drama—was unwilling to give his story so tragic a termination. This may perhaps be borne out by the subscription to the Bengali recension (Oster, p. 11): 'The poems of the approaching death of King Bhoja are not written here as being inauspicious . . . and so (only) the poems dealing with the glory of noble King Bhoja are written as heard.'

From these facts, which will receive additional confirmation (were any needed) when we consider the poets who, Ballāla says, adorned Bhoja's court (pp. 5-6, 98-102), it is evident that his narrative has no historical value whatever; the only one who has even suspected it to have the slightest worth in this respect seems to have been Lassen (iii, 836-855).

The account of Muñja and Bhoja given by Ballāla differs widely from those recorded by the Jain poet Rājavallabha in his *Bhojacaritra* (thus far extant only in manuscript; J. Tod, *Transactions of the Royal Asiatic*

Society of Great Britain and Ireland, i [1827], 218-225; H. T. Colebrooke, *ibid.*, pp. 228-229; *Catalogue of the Sanskrit and Prākrit Manuscripts in the Library of the India Office*, ii, Oxford, 1935, 1362 = no. 7656) and by the Jain Merutuṅga in his *Prabandhacintāmaṇi* (Taw., pp. 30-77). According to these two compositions (Tod, p. 219; Taw., pp. 56-57), as also according to an anonymous commentator on stanza 42 of Mānatuṅga's *Bhaktāmarastotra* (perhaps third or fourth century; cf. G. P. Quackenbos, *The Sanskrit Poems of Mayūra*, New York, 1917, pp. 16-18, 266), Bhoja was a convert to Jainism, although their accounts of the King's change of faith are irreconcilable. Against these may be set, for whatever it be worth, the direct statement of the Brāhman Govinda to Bhoja (P, p. 10): 'Sire, thou art a Vaiṣṇavite.' Though it is not impossible that, as Quackenbos says (pp. 42-49): 'The *Bhojaprabandha* . . . may be a work of Jain origin,' in itself it shows no evidence of such a source, but is strictly Brāhmanic throughout. The only arguments in favour of Jainism apparently are the statements of the Jain authors just mentioned (which may not be wholly free from sectarian bias), the undoubted dependence of Ballāla on the *Prabandhacintāmaṇi*, and—perhaps most cogent of all—a Sanskrit and Kanarese inscription from Śravaṇa Beḷgoḷa in Madras (Kielhorn, *Southern India*, no. 1022) 'giving an acount of some Jaina teachers among whom is a Prabhâchandra whose feet were worshipped by Bhojarâjâ, the king of Dhârâ.'

As counter-arguments, one may cite the replacement, in the *Bhojaprabandha*, of the tenth-century Śvetāmbara Jain Dhanapāla, a convert from Brāhmanism (Taw., pp. 52-58) and the author of the Sanskrit *kāvya Tilakamañjarī*, the Prākrit *Ṛṣabhapañcāśikā* in fifty stanzas honouring the first prophet of the Jains, and the oldest Prākrit lexicon, the *Pāiyalacchīnāmamālā* (Winternitz, ii, 336, 341; iii, 415), by Viṣṇu, Śākalya, and an unnamed poet from Jālandhara (*202* = Mer. 101; *216* = Mer. 95; *288* = Mer. 102), where Dhanapāla is ignored (in the Bengali recension, only stanza 194 = Mer. 93—not in the southern recension—is ascribed to him). In like manner, two stanzas attributed to the Jain Siddhasena in Mer. 11 are given to Jyotirīśvara Kaviśekhara in the *Bhojaprabandha* (*311, 318*); and one (*230*) assigned to him in Mer. 15 is by Bhoja's court-panegyrist according to Ballāla. It seems, therefore, by no means certain that Ballāla was in any way inclined to Jainism unless he deliberately slanted his book in favour of orthodox Brāhmanism.

Bhoja enjoyed the highest reputation in India not merely as a King and patron of letters, but also as an author in many fields: astronomy, medicine, *kāvya* (artificial and learned poetry), law, philosophy (especially Śaivite), lexicography, polity, architecture, poetics, and as a compiler of an anthology. Aufrecht (i, 418; ii, 95[b]; iii, 90[a]; cf. Winternitz, iii, 21, 375, 461) lists some twenty-five works, but says: 'It is almost superfluous to add that not one . . . were (*sic*) actually written by himself, but belong to authors who either lived during his reign, or some time after.' All that can with any degree of assurance be attributed to him are the *Sarasvatīkaṇṭhābharaṇa* on poetics, the *Śṛṅgāraprakāśa* on rhetoric (Krishnamachariar, pp. 750-751; Winternitz, iii, 21; Regnaud, p. 380; ed. V. Raghavan, Bombay, 1947 sqq.), and the first five books of the *kāvya Campūrāmāyaṇa* or *Rāmāyaṇacampū* (Aufrecht, i, 183; ii, 37[a]; iii, 39[a]; Krishnamachariar, pp. 503-504). Sanskrit anthologies ascribe to him some sixty stanzas (F. W. Thomas, *Kavīndravacanasamuccaya, a Sanskrit Anthology of Verses,* Calcutta, 1912, pp. 63-65), of which only three (*36, 185, 216*) are found in the *Bhojaprabandha.* In the *Vikramacarita* or *Siṁhāsanadvātriṁśikā* (edition and translation of all four recensions by F. Edgerton, 2 vols., Cambridge, Mass., 1926 = *Harvard Oriental Series,* xxvi-xxvii), Bhoja is the central figure, the original version probably being written in his honour and during his reign, and the Jain recension apparently being considerably later. Here Bhoja discovers the buried lion-throne of Vikramāditya adorned with thirty-two statuettes—who are in reality demi-goddesses under a curse—each of whom tells him a story. Until he can equal the nobility, generosity, and other virtues of Vikramāditya (cf. *179-180, 229, 231*), he is unable to ascend the throne; but at last he meets the test and the demi-goddesses, freed from their curse, return to heaven. The *Bhojaprabandha* stanzas *16, 28, 143, 144, 170, 240, 311,* and *313* are found also in the *Vikramacarita.*

Ballāla drew very largely on the *Prabandhacintāmaṇi,* the most evident direct borrowings being the *samasyā* between Bhoja and a Brāhman fording a stream with a load of wood and the entry of the King's gift in the religious account-book (*185, 190* = Mer. 66; Taw. 37-38); the *samasyā* in which the comptroller of the treasury (according to Mer., Rohaka, the prime minister) reproves Bhoja for his extravagant generosity (*198* = Mer. 66; Taw. 36-37); the episode of the freezing Brāhman (*232-233* = Mer. 73; Taw. 42); the colloquy between Bhoja and a thief (*236-237* = Mer. 67; Taw. 38); the sad fate of Māgha (*279, 281-283* = Mer. 86-87; Taw. 50-51); and the deciphering by Kālidāsa (B-P) or by Dhanapāla (Mer.) of an inscription found in the Narmadā (*306*) or in a temple of Śiva submerged under-sea (Mer. 99; Taw. 65).

The full list of these borrowings is as follows:

B-P stanzas	Mer. pp.	Taw. pp.
6	57	32
38	58	32
65	140	84
185	66	37-38
190	66	38
198	64	36-37
201	75	43
202	101	61
212	71	41
216	95	57
230	15, 68	12
231	68	39
232-234	73-74	42
236-237	67	38
279	86	80
281-283	87	51
288	102	62
306	99	60
309	72	41
311, 313	15	11

Oster also observes (p. 36) that, in borrowing, Ballāla frequently substitutes *Bhoja* for *rājan* ('O King!').

The *Bhopaprabandha* is, in essence, a pseudo-historical tale which provides a slight framework for mild adventures of Bhoja and his extravagant prodigality to poets in admiration of verses either written by them or ascribed to them—an extravagance so excessive that it compels his prime minister and his comptroller of the Royal treasury to protest against his wastefulness (pp. 24, 54-55, 57-58). It is, in short, a *quasi*-anthology. Some of the stanzas, taken from the *Pañcatantra, Hitopadeśa, Mahābhārata, Rāmāyaṇa,* Manu, etc. (e. g., *1-2*; *5*; *7*; *11*; *13-17*; *23*; *28*; *31-32*; *42-44*; *47*; *55*; *57*; *63*; *100*; *102*; *135*; *143*; *145*; *147*; *193*; *218*; *308*), are, in reality, no more plagiarisms than quotations from the Bible or Shakespeare would be in an English literary work.

How untrustworthy are the attributions of many stanzas to the poets to whom Ballāla ascribes them will be clear from the section on 'Poets Quoted in the *Bhojaprabandha*' (pp. 98-102); and Thomas (p. 17) very pertinently remarks, with regard to Sanskrit anthologies generally: 'In many cases the works cited vouch for a different authorship, or several different authorships.' Thus *51* = *140* is assigned in the one case to Govinda's father and in the other to Kālidāsa (a mere commonplace); *103* = *282* to Bāṇa and to Māgha; *186* = *314* to an anonymous Brāhman and to Kaviśekhara; perhaps also Sīmanta's recitation (*207*) from Bhartṛhari (i, 35) as his own composition. It is possible that at least some of these may be commonplaces which Ballāla merely puts in the poets' mouths; and the same very probably holds good of many another stanza ascribed in the *Bhojaprabandha* to one of the poets there mentioned, but by the anthologies to a different author or to different authors. Here Ballāla is neither much better nor much worse an authority than the professed anthologists. They are all alike open to considerable suspicion; their most truthful attribution, in many cases, is to 'somebody' (*kasyacit*). On the other hand, Ballāla betrays inexcusable ignorance or the grossest carelessness when he makes Bhoja reward Sīmanta (*240*) for an obvious plagiarism from Subandhu's *Vāsavadattā* 11 (ascribed to Bāṇa in the Bengali recension).

The latest poet named in the *Bhojaprabandha* to whom a date may even approximately be assigned is Jyotirīśvara Kaviśekhara (*310-314*) late in the fifteenth century, the author of the farce (*prahasana*) *Dhūrtasamāgama* (Konow, pp. 115-116); and the single explicit citation (*306*) is from the *Hanumannāṭaka* or *Mahānāṭaka* (xiv, 43), written probably between the tenth and the fourteenth century (Konow, pp. 88-90; Winternitz, iii, 242-244). Here the utter lack of chronological sense is shown (as it is in its source, Mer. 99; Taw. 60) when the missing half of the stanza is correctly supplied by Kālidāsa (probably end of the fourth and beginning of the fifth century) after unsuccessful attempts by Bhoja (eleventh century) and Bhavabhūti (first half of the eighth century). It is equally absurd to find at Bhoja's court in the eleventh century such poets as Kālidāsa of the fourth and fifth century, Bāṇa, Daṇḍin, Mayūra, and Māgha of the seventh, Bhavabhūti of the eighth, and Jyotirīśvara Kaviśekhara of the late fifteenth. With regard to the numerous stanzas ascribed to Kālidāsa, A. F. R. Hoernle (*Journal of the Royal Asiatic Society,* 1906, pp. 699-700) has very plausibly suggested that the name may have served merely as a peg on which to hang them. Krishnamachariar's supposition (p. 164) that the Kālidāsa of the *Bhojaprabandha* may have been Padmagupta, who flourished in the last quarter of the tenth century and the first of the eleventh, the author of the *Navasāhasāṅkacarita,* and also called Parimala(kālidāsa), seems scarcely tenable; nor is it any more likely that some of the stanzas ascribed to him were really by some one of the poets called Abhinava-kālidāsa or Navakālidāsa.

The prose of the *Bhojaprabandha* is, for the most part, quite simple, even when Ballāla occasionally launches out briefly in an attempt at 'fine writing.' Of the poems, four (*136, 184, 319, 321*), not assigned to any author, may conceivably be Ballāla's own compositions; in any case, they reveal scant poetic genius.

In many cases, the poets to whom the *Bhojaprabandha* ascribes stanzas are shamelessly obsequious fawners, not to say outright beggars (e. g., *66-67*; *69-71*; *76*; *79-80*; *82-85*; *92*; *116-120*; *123*; *127*; *130-132*; *162*; *165-167*; *172-173*; *176*; *181-183*; *185-187*; *195*; *197*; *202*; *208-210*; *212-214*; *216-218*; *220-221*; *225-227*; *230*; *234*; *236*; *238-239*; *241*; *256*; *264*; *266-267*; *272*; *275*; *289*; *300*; *308*; *310-314*; *316*; *324*).

Śleṣas (paronomasias), indicated in this translation by < > and so frequent in Sanskrit *kāvya*, are entirely absent from Ballāla's prose, but occur in several of the stanzas which he quotes: *60* (Bhoja's prime minister); *67* (a Kaliṅga poet); *138* (Līlāvatī); *141* (Bāṇa); *142* (second half; Kālidāsa); *301, 303, 326-327* (Kālidāsa); *230* (court-panegyrist); *235* (Mayūra); *243* (Dharmadatta in V; to a poet from Puṣkara in Ajmere according to the Bengali recension; anonymous in B-P); *247* (Bāṇa's son); *249, 251* (Bhavabhūti); *268* (Devajaya); *310-311* (Kaviśekhara).

Samasyās (verse-cappings; cf. note 94) are found in *75* (Śaṅkara and Bhoja); *86* (two poetasters and Kālidāsa); *112*; *142*; *154*; *258*; *265*; *292*; *294-296*; *302-303*; *317* (Bhoja and Kālidāsa); *161* (Bhoja, Bāṇa, Maheśvara, and Kālidāsa); *168-171* (Bhoja and a learned Brāhman's family); *182* (Bhoja and a hunter's wife); *185* (Bhoja and a Brāhman); *198* (Bhoja's prime minister and Bhoja); *200, 236* (Bhoja and thieves); *293* (Bhoja and Bhavabhūti); *304-306* (Bhavabhūti, Bhoja, and Kālidāsa); *307* (a Brahmarākṣasa and Kālidāsa); *320* (Bhoja, Bhavabhūti, Daṇḍin, and Kālidāsa); *322* (Aśvins and Kālidāsa).

Two works of interest here (both thus far known in manuscript only) seem to be the tenth-century *Kavisamayavilāsa* of Revaṇārādhya and the fifteenth-century *Rājaśekharacarita* of Kavikuñjara. The first of these is a collection of humorous tales about the poets at Bhoja's court; and the second, in scheme closely resembling the *Bhojaprabandha,* but with its hero Rājaśekhara, King of Vijayanagara (1479-1483; Duff, pp. 263, 309; the eleventh-century date given by Krishnamachariar, p. 506, is scarcely correct), 'generally inculcating morals, collects stories said to have been narrated by Rasikaśekhara, a pupil of Abhinavakālidāsa, to his friend Subuddhi, quoting fine verses of Navīnakālidāsa and other poets of King Rājaśekhara's Court' (Krishnamachariar, pp. 503; 431-432, 508-511).

Bhojaprabandhas are also attributed to Merutuṅga (the author of the *Prabandhacintāmaṇi*), Vatsarāja, the Śvetāmbara Jain Śubhaśīlagaṇi (fifteenth century), and Padmagupta. There are likewise an epitome of Ballāla's work, the *Bhojaprabandhasāra*, and an anonymous *kāvya*, the *Bhojarājavijaya*—all in manuscript only except the composition of Padmagupta, which is mentioned solely in the introduction to the *Yuktikalpataru*, treating of practical life and political government, and ascribed to Bhoja himself (Aufrecht, i, 476[a]; Krishnamachariar, p. 502; ed. Īśvara Candra Śāstri, Calcutta, 1917; this statement in itself renders Bhoja's authorship of the *Yuktikalpataru* highly improbable). According to the seventeenth-century anthologist Harikavi, the dramatist Rājaśekhara, who flourished at the end of the ninth and the beginning of the tenth century, also wrote a *Bhojaprabandha* (Krishnamachariar, p. 388, note 1). If so—and we have already observed that ascriptions by anthologists are only too frequently open to doubt—this Bhoja cannot, for chronological reasons, have been the King of Dhārā. There is also a drama, of unknown date and authorship, the *Bhojarājataraṅgiṇī*, recorded solely in the list of the library of Kavīndrācārya in the seventeenth century (Krishnamachariar, p. 390c), as well as the nineteenth-century one-act *Bhojarājāñka* of Sundara Vīrarāghava, describing Muñja's conspiracy against Bhoja's life (Krishnamachariar, pp. 501, note, 667); but the two-act *Bhoja(rāja)saccarita* of Vedāntavāgīśa Bhaṭṭācārya is not concerned with Ballāla's hero (Konow, p. 110).

The manuscripts of the *Bhojaprabandha* fall into two classes: South Indian and Bengali. All the printed texts, except T. Pavie's (autographed) belong to the first group. Unfortunately, Pavie's edition of the Bengali recension (*Bhôdjaprabandha, histoire de Bhôdja, roi de Mâlwa et des paṇḍites de son temps, par Ballala,* Paris, 1855) is so uncritical that it is almost useless (Oster, pp. 6-8), and the same statement holds true of his text and translation of the first section (P, 1-9) under the same title (*Journal asiatique,* V, iii [1854], 185-230) and of his translation of some passages ('Le Poëte Kâlidâsa à la cour de Bhôdja, roi de Malwa' and 'Les Paṇḍits à la cour du roi Bhôdja,' *ibid.*, iv [1854], 385-431; v [1855], 76-105). Of this Bengali recension there is an edition of the first section, with the variants of thirteen manuscripts, by Oster (pp. 38-61), whose work has never been carried further. Since, then, no reliable text of this recension has thus far been printed (even Pavie's edition is rare), and since Oster's dissertation may not be generally accessible, his account of the differences between the two versions (pp. 9-15) may be summarised, especially as we know practically nothing about these divergencies except what he tells us. Of necessity this translation is based throughout on the South Indian recension.

The older recension seems to be the Bengali, which has by far the better readings, while the South Indian has been much interpolated, but is more careful stylistically. The South Indian alone has the colloquy between Bhoja and Kālidāsa with the stanzas on the might of love (P, 16. 6-17. 3); the weighing of the poems of Kālidāsa and Bhavabhūti in a balance in Pārvatī's temple (56. 6-26); the stanzas of the King and Kālidāsa on Bhoja's chowry-bearer, the miraculous saving of a child that had fallen into the fire, Kālidāsa's and Bhavabhūti's capping of a *samasyā* proposed by Bhoja, a stanza by Kālidāsa, the episode of the unfaithful wife, three stanzas on a girl playing at ball, the stanza of Śivaśarman, Kālidāsa's stanza on a fire-vessel, and his completion of two more *samasyās* (65. 25-70. 20); Bhoja's illness and his healing by the Aśvins (76. 13-78. 15); and Kālidāsa's displeasure at Bhoja and their reconciliation (79. 13-80. 5).

The Bengali recension, on the other hand, is the only one to narrate the arrival at the Royal court of a young Brāhman to whom Bhoja had given a gift on the way (ed. Pavie, p. 59); the story of Malayasiṁha and Vijaya (pp. 61-65); an Apabhraṁśa Prākrit stanza on an elephant (p. 67); Bhoja's stanza on a rain-cloud (pp. 71-72); a long section (pp. 74-77) containing a hunting-scene between the King and Dhanapāla; Dāmodara's stanza on the sandal-powder on Bhoja's person (cf. *220*); a poet's strophe on a rain-cloud, and a night-adventure of a poor Brāhman family with a kind-hearted thief; a brief story of a poet from Puṣkara (cf. *242-243* and note 169) and another of like type (pp. 104-105); Kālidāsa's meeting with robbers skilled in art (p. 105); and the same poet's stanzas just before going to the land of Ballāla (pp. 110-111; cf. P, p. 62). According to this recension, moreover, before Kālidāsa determines the reading of the stanza (*306*) from the *Hanumannāṭaka*, the court-poets also indulge (cf. P, pp. 70-71) in conjectures which are proved false by inspection of a temple of Śiva discovered lying under the surface of the sea (p. 121).

ABBREVIATIONS

(Works mentioned only once are not listed here, but at the places where they are cited.)

Aufrecht: Theodor Aufrecht, *Catalogus Catalogorum: An Alphabetical Register of Sanskrit Works and Authors*, 3 vols., Leipzig, 1891-1903.

B-P: *Bhojaprabandha*, ed. P.

Duff: C. Mabel Duff, *The Chronology of India from the Earliest Times to the Beginning of the Sixteenth Century*, Westminster, 1899.

Haeberlin: John Haeberlin, *Kávya-Sangraha: A Sanscrit Anthology, Being a Collection of the Best Smaller Poems in the Sanscrit Language*, Calcutta, 1847.

Hopkins: Edward Washburn Hopkins, *Epic Mythology*, Strasbourg, 1915.

IS: Otto von Böhtlingk, *Indische Sprüche*, 2d ed., 3 vols., Petrograd, 1870-73.

Jolly, *Medicin*: Julius Jolly, [*Indische*] *Medicin*, Strasbourg, 1901.

Jolly, *Recht*: Julius Jolly, [*Indische*] *Recht und Sitte*, Strasbourg, 1896.

Konow: Sten Konow, *Das indische Drama*, Berlin and Leipzig, 1920.

Krishnamachariar: M. Krishnamachariar, *History of Classical Sanskrit Literature*, Madras, 1937.

Lassen: Christian Lassen, *Indische Alterthumskunde*, 4 vols., Leipzig, 1857-74 (vols. i and ii in 2d ed.).

Macdonell: Arthur Anthony Macdonell, *Vedic Mythology*, Strasbourg, 1897.

Mer.: Merutuṅga's *Prabandhacintāmaṇi*, ed. Rāmacandra Dīnānātha, Bombay, 1888.

Oster: Ludwig Oster, *Die Rezensionen des Bhojaprabandha*, Darmstadt, 1911 (Heidelberg dissertation).

P: *The Bhojaprabandha of Ballāla*, ed. Kāśīnāth Pāṇḍuraṅg Parab, 2d ed., Bombay, 1904; ed. Vāsudeva Lakṣmaṇa Paṇaśīkar, 10th ed., Bombay, 1932 (a reprint of the preceding with correction of most of the misprints).

Regnaud: Paul Regnaud, *La Rhétorique sanskrite*, Paris, 1884.

Sad.: Śrīdharadāsa's *Saduktikarṇāmṛta* (1205), ed. Rāmāvatāra Śarmā, Lahore, 1933.

Śārṅ.: *Paddhati* of Śārṅgadhara (1363), ed. Peter Peterson, i (all published), Bombay, 1888.

Schmidt: Richard Schmidt, *Beiträge zur indischen Erotik*, Leipzig, 1902.

Subhāṣ: *Subhāṣitāvalī* of Vallabhadeva (15th century?), ed. Peter Peterson and Durgāprasāda, Bombay, 1886.

Sūk: *Sūktimuktāvalī* of Bhagadatta Jalhaṇa (13th century), ed. Embar Krishnamacharya, Baroda, 1938.

T: edition of the *Bhojaprabandha* in Telugu characters, Madras, 1927.

Taw.: C. H. Tawney's tr. of Merutuṅga's *Prabandhacintāmaṇi*, Calcutta, 1901.

V: *Bhojaprabandha*, ed. (with excellent modern commentary) Āśubodha Vidyābhūṣaṇa and Nityabodha Vidyāratna, 2d ed., Calcutta, 1923.

Vikrama.: *Vikrama's Adventures* (*Vikramacarita, Siṁhāsanadvātriṁśika*), ed. and tr. F. Edgerton, 2 vols., Cambridge, Mass., 1926; SR: Southern Recension; JR: Jain Recension; MR: Metrical Recension.

Wilson: Horace Hayman Wilson, *Select Specimens of the Theatre of the Hindus*, 2 vols., 2d ed., London, 1835.

Winternitz: Moritz Winternitz, *Geschichte der indischen Litteratur*, 3 vols., Leipzig, 1908-23 (?).

Yule-Burnell: Henry Yule and Arthur C. Burnell, *Hobson-Jobson*, new ed. by William Crooke, London, 1903.

( ): words added to clarify the meaning in English; in the list of poets, identifications and names of poets to whom stanzas are ascribed in Vikrama and anthologies differing from the ascriptions in B-P.

[ ]: enclosing numerals, the pagination in P; enclosing words, equivalents of terms which might be obscure, but are too brief to warrant special footnotes; in the list of poets, identifications, etc., for names enclosed in parentheses.

⟨ ⟩: enclosing paronomasias.

*: prefixed to a word or meaning in the lexicographical appendix when such word or meaning is cited in Otto Böhtlingk's *Sanskrit-Wörterbuch in kürzerer Fassung*, 7 parts, Petrograd, 1879-89, or in Richard Schmidt's *Nachträge zum Sanskrit-Wörterbuch in kürzerer Fassung von Otto Böhtlingk*, Leipzig, 1928, only on the authority of native lexicographers.

°: prefixed to a word or meaning in the lexicographical appendix when such word or meaning is entirely omitted by Böhtlingk and Schmidt.

THE BHOJAPRABANDHA OF BALLĀLA

[*1*] Hail! Of the glorious great King-Emperor Bhojarāja the tale is told.

In the beginning, in the Kingdom of Dhārā a King named Sindhula long protected (his) subjects. In his old age a son Bhoja was born. When he (was) five years old, then (his) father, knowing his own agedness, summoning (his) chief ministers, perceiving (his) younger brother Muñja (to be) very mighty, and seeing (his) son (to be but) a child, reflected: 'If, disregarding (my) uterine brother, capable of bearing the burden of the splendour of a King, I give the Kingdom to (my) son, then (there will be) reproach from folk; or even, out of greed for the Kingdom, Muñja will slay my young son by poison and the like. Then the Kingdom (will have been) given in vain; and loss of a son (is) extirpation of lineage.

> 'Greed (is) the foundation of evil, and greed, in sooth, (its) procreator; greed, the parent of hatred, wrath, and the like, (is) the cause of evil. (1)
>
> 'From greed anger cometh, from anger injury ariseth; through injury a wise man, even knowing the *śāstras*, goeth to hell. (2)[1]
>
> 'Possessed by greed, a man slayeth mother, father, or brother most dear, or a lord uterine.' (3)

So thinking (and) giving the Kingdom to Muñja, he left his own son Bhoja in his lap.

Then, the King gone to heaven in due course, Muñja, gaining possession of the Kingdom (and) dismissing the prime minister, named Buddhisāgara, with (his) seal of office, appointed another in his place. Then he has the King's son recite to teachers. Then in due course, in the court a Brāhman (who had) crossed to the farther shore of astronomy (and who was) skilled in all sciences, coming and saying 'Hail' to the King, took (his) seat. And he said: 'Sire, this folk sayeth (that) I (am) omniscient. So ask me somewhat.

> 'Knowledge that may be on the tip of one's tongue[2] should always be manifested by the wise; a fool is deceived by knowledge which (is only) in a teacher (or) a book.' (4)

So he spoke to the King. Then the King, hearing that news, amazing because of the Brāhman's stamp of self-esteem, said: 'If thou tellest

[1] Cf. IS 5882-5883.

[2] Lit., 'standing in the throat.'

every single thing, whatsoever practised by me (and) whatsoever done from our birth until this moment, [*2*] Thine Honour (is) indeed omniscient.' Then the Brāhman told every single thing whatsoever that (had been) done by the King, even a secret action. Then the King, knowing all the tokens, was pleased. And again going five (or) six paces, falling at (the Brāhman's) feet (and) seating him on the lion-throne inlaid with sapphires, topazes, emeralds, (and) cat's-eyes, the King said:

> 'Like a mother she protecteth, like a father she directeth unto weal, and like a wife she doth delight, removing affliction; and in the world doth she spread fame unspotted (and) good fortune. What doth not knowledge, like the Kalpalatā,[3] make to prosper?' (5)

Then he gave the most excellent Brāhman ten horses of noble stock.

Then, seated in the court, Buddhisāgara addressed the King: 'Sire, ask the Brāhman Bhoja's horoscope.' Then said Muñja: 'Cast Bhoja's horoscope.' Then the Brāhman said: 'Bhoja should be brought from the study-hall.' Then, out of curiosity, Muñja had Bhoja, adorning the study-hall, brought by soldiers from the study-hall. Then, clearly bowing down to the King as (his) father, he stood modestly. Then, the circle of princes confounded by the beauty of (his) appearance, the astrologer, considering Bhoja, with exceeding good fortune like great Indra come to earth's circle, with a figure like the God of Love, like Good Fortune incarnate, said to the King: 'O King, even Viriñci [Brahmā] (were) unable to tell the rise of Bhoja's prosperity; who (am) I, a gluttonous Brāhman,[4] (to do this)? Even so, I say somewhat according to (mine) understanding. Send Bhoja hence to the study-hall.' Then, Bhoja gone to the study-hall at the King's command, the Brāhman said:

> 'Fifty years (and) five, seven months, (and) three days the Deccan with Gauḍa (is) to be enjoyed by Bhoja.' (6)[5]

Hearing this, (though) cleverly laughing (it) off, as it were, (and) with a cheerful countenance, the King became pale of face. Then, dismissing the Brāhman, going to bed at midnight, the King reflected alone: 'If Royal fortune shall come to Prince Bhoja, then even (though) living, I (am) dead.

[3] Cf. IS 4807; to Trivikrama in Vikrama. SR ix, 5. The Kalpalatā, also called *kalpataru* in stanza 197, fabled to fulfil all desires, is one of the five trees of Indra's paradise.

[4] Cf. the conventional *vidūṣaka* of the Sanskrit drama. The humility is, of course, feigned.

[5] = Mer. 57 (Taw. 32); cf. above, p. 1; Gauḍa here means all North India.

'Those (same) unimpaired senses, even that (same) name, that (same) uninjured intellect, that (same) voice—[3] a man deserted by the glow of wealth straightway becometh another; strange (is) this! (7)[6]

'And, moreover:

'Naught is hard to do for a man careless of (his) body, dexterous, resolute, (and) with (his) purpose begun with understanding. (8)

'Through previous means and efforts, and with friends and counsellors, the success of doers is gained even by one smitten with jealousy. (9)

'In that effort what (is) hard to be accomplished?

'Far (away), step by step, go the successes of men possessed of exceeding dexterity, (but) apprehensive (and) fearful of the reproach of others. (10)

'And, moreover:

'Time drinketh the success of taking, of giving, and of a deed to be done, (but) not done quickly. (11)[7]

'Putting disrespect before and respect behind, a wise man would uphold his own interest; ruin of one's own interest (is) folly. (12)[8]

'Not for the sake of a very little thing would a man of understanding destroy much; this, indeed, (is) exceeding wisdom, since from a very little thing destruction of much (may come). (13)[9]

'He who quelleth not an enemy or a disease just born is later killed thereby, even (though) exceeding stout of limb. (14)[10]

'What will enemies combined do to (one whose) body (is) protected by wisdom, like water-torrents to an umbrella held in the hand? (15)[11]

'A sagacious (man) should not undertake matters fruitless, with ill outcome and (with) fruits of equal loss (and gain), and impossible.' (16)[12]

And then, thus reflecting, in the third night-watch of the day,[13] taking counsel all alone, he sent his own body-guard to summon Vatsarāja, the very mighty over-lord of Vaṅga [Bengal].[14] And that body-guard, approaching Vatsarāja, said: 'The King summoneth thee.' Then, mounting (his) chariot, coming surrounded by (his) retinue, perceiving

[6] = IS 2533; ascribed to Kṣemendra in Sūk. cxxv, 6; to an anonymous Brāhman in Vikrama. SR xxi, 8.

[7] = IS 938.

[8] = IS 400.

[9] = IS 3506; to the eighteenth statuette in Vikrama. SR xviii, 5.

[10] Cf. IS 2380.

[11] Cf. IS 4210.

[12] = IS 479; anonymous in Vikrama. SR xx; 2; JR xx, 3.

[13] Between midnight and 3 A. M.

[14] I have found no other mention of this monarch.

the King, (and) doing obeisance, he seated himself. And the King, emptying the palace, said to Vatsarāja:

> [4] 'A King, even (when) pleased, giveth only honour to (his) subjects; but they, being honoured, serve him even with (their) lives. (17)[15]

'So in the first watch of the night Bhoja must be killed by thee in the forest of Bhuvaneśvarī[16] and (his) head brought to the Royal palace.' And he [Vatsarāja], rising up (and) bowing to the Prince, said: '(My) Lord's commands (are my) standard; (yet) even so, I desire to say somewhat with Thy Majesty's indulgence; then let my speech be suffered, even (though) wrong.

> 'In Bhoja (is) neither wealth nor army nor mighty retinue, but like a youngling he sitteth to-day. Why should he be killed, O King? (18)
>
> 'Clinging to thy feet like a successor (and) gluttonous—in his death I see no reason, Bull of Kings.' (19)

Then the King narrated the whole event (which had) taken place in the court in the morning. And he [Vatsarāja], hearing (it), said, laughing:

> 'Rāma is lord of the triple world; Vasiṣṭha, Brahmā's son;[17] by him [Vasiṣṭha] the (auspicious) moment in (Rāma's) consecration to the Kingdom was told. (20)
>
> 'By that moment even Rāma was led landless to the forest, (and) the abduction of Sītā took place; vain (was) Viriñci's [Brahmā's] word. (21)
>
> 'Who (is) this wight, Best of Kings, little-knowing (and) gluttonous, by whose word thou wishest to kill a Prince with Love's (own) form? (22)

'And, moreover:

> '"What would be mine doing this, or what would be mine doing it not?" Hereon reflecting with thought, a prudent (man) would either do or not. (23)[18]
>
> 'By a wise man performing an aggregate of activities usual or unusual the consequences should carefully be considered; the ripening of deeds done with excessive haste becometh disaster, heart-burning (and) dart-like. (24)

'And, moreover:

> 'How, even (on the part) of evil men, doth memory cease till death regarding him with whom one hath sat, eaten, laughed, and talked confidentially in private? (25)

---

[15] = IS 5754.

[16] 'Mistress of the World' is here a synonym of Mahāmāyā (Durgā), see below, p. 17.

[17] For Vasiṣṭha and other 'mental sons' of Brahmā see Hopkins, pp. 189-190.

[18] Cf. IS 1762.

'And, moreover, he [Bhoja] being killed, old King Sindhula's vessels of exceeding affection, mighty heroes, (and) standing even in thine esteem, will inundate thy city like clouds with dashing billows. [*5*] Even (though) thou (hast) long been firmly rooted, belike the citizens will make Bhoja lord of earth. And, moreover:

> 'And if, in (the case of) an action well done (in principle), the execution (be) bad, this itself taketh away (its) glory; the whirlwind rendeth asunder the flame of the lamp, (even though) always supplied with oil. (26)

'Sire, the slaying of a son nowhere (worketh) for weal.' The King, hearing Vatsarāja's word thus spoken, said, angered: 'Thou thyself (art) lord of a Kingdom, not a servant.

> 'He who striveth not for (what hath been) said by (his) lord is a slave, the basest of slaves; his life (is) in vain, like the two teats on a goat's neck.' (27)

Then Vatsarāja was silent, thinking: 'I must consider a convenient season.'

Then at setting sun, seeing Vatsarāja descending from the roof of the lofty palace like angry Death, the assembled courtiers, terrified, gained their homes under various pretexts. Then, sending his servants to guard his house (and) turning (his) chariot toward the temple of Bhuvaneśvarī, Vatsarāja sent one to summon Prince Bhoja's teacher. And he [the messenger] said to the paṇḍit: 'Father, Vatsarāja summoneth thee.' Hearing this, as though struck by a thunderbolt, as though entered by a demon, as though seized by Graha,[19] the paṇḍit (was) brought by the servant, holding (him) by the hand. And the prudent Vatsarāja said to him with an obeisance: 'Paṇḍit, father, sit down. Bring the victorious Royal Prince from the study-hall.' Asking the conquering Prince (as he was) coming something (that he had) studied, he brought (him). Again he [Vatsarāja] said to the paṇḍit: 'Brāhman, bring Prince Bhoja.' Then, knowing the affair, Bhoja arriving angered, blazing, so to speak, (and) with eyes of blood, said: 'Knave, what, in sooth, is thy power to bring forth from the Royal palace only me, the King's chief Prince?' With these words, Vatsarāja (was) struck in the region of the palate by Bhoja, taking (his) shoe from (his) left foot. Then said Vatsarāja: 'Bhoja, we (are) doing the King's bidding.' Making the child enter a chariot (and) drawing (his) sword, he went quickly to the temple of Mahāmāyā.[20]

[19] The 'Seizer,' one of a group of demons who 'seize' the body and soul of man, causing insanity, etc.

[20] Cf. note 16.

Then, Bhoja seized, the folk made a tumult, and an uproar arose. Saying, 'What! What!' the soldiers shouting, coming precipitately, (and) knowing (that) Bhoja (was) led to death, entering the elephant-stable, the camel-stable, the horse-stable, (and) the chariot-stable, killed them all. Then in the streets, on the balconies of the ramparts of the King's palace, on the tops of the outer gates, in the environs of the city, the sky was mocked by the din of the noise of kettle-drums, tabors, tambourines, *maḍḍukas,* (and) *diṇḍimas.* Some [6] abandoned (their) lives by the bright sword, some by poison, some by the spear, some by the noose, some by fire, some by the axe, some by the crescent-headed arrow, some by the javelin, some by the dart, some by water, some in the stream—wives of Brāhmans, sons of Kings, servants of Kings, Kings, and citizens.

Then Bhoja's mother, named Sāvitrī, being, so to speak, the mother of all, hearing of her son's plight from a slave-girl's mouth, covering (her) eyes with (her) hands, said, weeping: '(My) son, to what a state hast thou come through (thy) father's brother! Vain for me to-day (have) become the penances and fasts performed by me for thy sake! The faces of the ten quarters (of the sky are) empty! (My) son, (our) glories (are) wiped away by God, omniscient (and) omnipotent![21] (My) son, behold this throng of slave-girls, (their) heads suddenly cloven!' With these words, she fell to the ground.

Then, the (evening-)fire kindled, the sky soiled, as it were, by the mass of smoke (that had) arisen, (and) the disk of the sun sunk in the western sea as though from terror of evil, Vatsarāja, come to the temple of Mahāmāyā, said to Bhoja: 'Prince, divinity of (thy) subjects, thine attainment of the Kingdom announced by a Brāhman skilled in astronomy, Thy Highness's death (hath been) ordered by the King.' Bhoja said:

> 'Reflecting on exile in (the case of) Rāma, on Bali's subjugation, on the forest of Pāṇḍu's sons, on the destruction of Vṛṣṇi's stock, on Prince Nala's fall from a Kingdom, on abiding in prison and meditation on death in (the case of) Laṅkā's lord [Rāvaṇa], every man perisheth by the will of Fate; who protecteth him? (28)[22]

---

[21] This seems to have a distinctly Muḥammadan flavour; cf. such phrases as *'innahu 'alīmu*ⁿ *qadīru*ⁿ ('Lo, He [God] (is) wise, mighty'), Qur'ān xlii, 49.

[22] Cf. IS 5782; to an anonymous Brāhman in Vikrama. SR iii, 12. The Kaustubha jewel and the Pārijāta tree were obtained at the Churning of the Ocean by the gods and demons; Rāma suffered exile for fourteen years before ascending the throne of Ayodhyā (Oudh), and his wife Sītā was abducted by Rāvaṇa (cf. stanzas 20, 21); for Bali see note 146; the five sons of Pāṇḍu (the Pāṇḍavas) escaped the plot against them by their cousin Duryodhana and sought refuge in a

'The son of the nectar-ocean [the moon], born together with Lakṣmī, Kaustubha, and the Pārijāta, by way of affection (and) favour (is) borne on (his) head by the god Śambhu [Śiva]; (but) even to-day the friend of night [the moon] escapeth not the waning decreed by Fate—by whom else is the course of Destiny, attended by a line upon a stone, transgressed? (29)[23]

'Wandering in the dreadful earth, climbing of a mountain, crossing of the ocean, a fetter, entry into a cave—how inescapable (is) the ripening of Fate! (30).

'Honour to that god [Fate], addicted to wayward marvels in (his) sport, by whose will the ocean becometh dry land, dry land an ocean, a bit of dust a mountain, Meru an atom of earth, a blade of grass a thunderbolt, a thunderbolt a blade of grass, fire coldness, (and) winter fieriness!' (31)[24]

Then, taking a leaf of a fig-tree, folding (it), cutting (his) leg with a knife, making the blood mount there in the fold, (and) writing a stanza on the leaf with a blade of grass, he [Bhoja] said to Vatsa: [7] '(Thou) of great fortune, this leaf (is) to be given to the King. Perform the King's command.' Then Vatsarāja's younger brother, perceiving the shining beauty of Bhoja's face at the moment of (his) abandonment of life, said:

'(There is) just one friend, Dharma, who followeth even in death; all else goeth to destruction together with the body. (32)[25]

'Neither father, mother, nor wife abideth then for companionship, neither son, friend, nor lineage; Dharma alone abideth. (33)

'Though mighty, (he is) powerless, though rich, devoid of wealth, and though learned, a fool—the wight who (hath his) face turned from Dharma. (34)

'What will that sick man do, come to a state (for which there is) no remedy, who maketh not leechcraft even here (in this world) for the disease of hell? (35)

'Wise (is) he who knoweth eld, death, fear, (and) disease; independent, would he stand or sit or sleep (or) laugh with any one? (36)

'(His) equals in lineage, age, and beauty (one) seeth taken away by Death; not even there is terror for thee; thy heart (is) like a thunderbolt.' (37)

Then Vatsarāja, developing a loathing (for his mission), saying, 'Be patient' to Bhoja, making obeisance to him, and having (him) enter a chariot, making (him) go in the thick darkness outside the city and

forest; most of Vṛṣṇi's descendants perished when Kṛṣṇa's capital, Dvārakā in Gujarat, was submerged by the ocean soon after his death; Nala lost his Kingdom playing at dice; Rāvaṇa, the demon King of Laṅkā (Ceylon), was taken prisoner by Kārtavīrya, King of the Haihayas.

[23] Cf. IS 5782; ascribed to Kṣemendra in Sūk. cxii, 4.

[24] = IS 545; ascribed to Kṣemendra in Sūk. cxii, 1; Subhāṣ. 3152.

[25] = IS 1345.

putting (him) in an underground chamber, guarded Bhoja. He himself, having (men) skilled in factitious arts make a head of Prince Bhoja with fair ear-rings, a twitching face, (and) closed eyes, taking it, (and) going with (his) younger brother to the King's palace, said, bowing to the King: 'What (was) commanded by the Illustrious One (hath been) fulfilled.' And then the King, knowing the killing of the child, said to him: 'Vatsarāja, what (was) said by the child at the instant of the sword-stroke?' Vatsa gave (him) the leaf. The King, having a lamp brought by the hand of his wife, reads the words on the leaf:

> 'Māndhātṛ, lord of earth, (that had) become the adornment of the Kṛta Age, (is) gone; where (is) that ten-mouthed one's [Rāvaṇa's] destroyer [Rāma], by whom the bridge (was) built in the Great Ocean? And others also, Yudhiṣṭhira and the rest, (are) gone to heaven, O Lord of Earth; with none whomsoever (hath) Earth gone; will she go with thee, O Muñja?' (38)[26]

And the King, knowing the meaning of this, fell from (his) couch to the ground. And then, restored to consciousness by the wind of the border of a garment agitated by the Queen's lotus-hand, (and) wailing like an osprey: 'O Queen, touch me not! Alas! Alas! A child-slayer!' summoning the door-keepers, he said: 'Fetch Brāhmans!' [*8*] Then, doing obeisance to the Brāhmans come together at his command, and saying: 'A child (hath been) slain by me. Tell (me) the expiation thereof!' they said: 'O King, enter the fire forthwith!'[27] Then Buddhisāgara, come with (them), said: 'As thou (art) the lowest of Kings, even so (is) Vatsarāja the lowest of prime ministers. Having given the Kingdom just to thee, Bhoja (was) placed in thy lap by King Sindhula; and that other thing [iniquity] (hath been) done by thee, (his) paternal uncle.

> 'In youth, lasting (but) a few days (and) intoxicating, the evil-souled commit iniquity so that even birth becometh in vain. (39)
>
> 'The good regard the removal of a blade of grass from the head (as equal to) a gift of a crore[28] of gold; evil men, forsooth, (though) benefited at the cost of life, (being) enemies, bear (this as) hostility. (40)
>
> 'Of the stony-hearted of whom benefit and injury are forgotten the phrase "he liveth" (is used) in vain. (41)

---

[26] = IS 4831 = Mer. 58 (Taw. 32). The Kṛta Age is the first and best of the four ages of the world. Rāma, the victor over Rāvaṇa, built a bridge (now known as Adam's Bridge) between India and Ceylon to conquer the island; Yudhiṣṭhira, the eldest of the Pāṇḍavas, was distinguished for his justice and rectitude.

[27] On suicide as expiation for murder see Jolly, *Recht*, pp. 118-119.

[28] 10,000,000.

'As a shoot, though very small, would become fruitful in time (if) protected with care, so (do) folk if (well) protected. (42)

'Gold, grain, jewels, and divers (kinds of) wealth, like everything else (belonging to) Lords of Earth, should be for (their) subjects. (43)[29]

'As the King, so the subjects: he virtuous, they (are) most virtuous; he evil, always they (are) most evil; they follow the King.' (44)[30]

Then at night, the King resolved on entering the fire, all the vassals and citizens assembled, (and) the rumour arose: 'Having slain the child, the King, terrified by terror at (his) sin, entereth the fire.' Then Buddhisāgara, summoning the door-keeper (and) saying: 'The King's palace is not to be entered by anyone,' having the King go into the citadel, sat down alone in the court. Then, hearing the report of the King's death, Vatsarāja, going to the council-hall (and) bowing to Buddhisāgara, said softly: 'Father, Bhojarāja (is) protected by me.' And Buddhisāgara said something in his ear; and Vatsarāja, hearing that, went out.

Then presently a Śaivite ascetic came to the court holding in (his) hand a staff of the tusk of a lordly elephant, with a newly made knot of braided hair, (his) whole body smeared with ashes mixed with camphor, like the God of Love in bodily form, [*9*] his ears adorned with crystal ear-rings, with a silken loin-cloth, like the Moon-Crested One [Śiva] in bodily form. Seeing him, Buddhisāgara said: 'Best of ascetics, whence hast thou come, and where thine abode? Thou (being) a Śaivite ascetic, thine amazing skill is specialty in medicine.' The ascetic said:

'In every place a dwelling, in every dwelling, too, food by alms, in lake and river water, O Śiva, Śiva! for men devoted to Truth. (45)

'In every village a lovely hut, in every waterfall water, and food in alms easy to get; what need of wealth? (46)

'Sire, we have no single place; (over) all earth's circle we wander; in (our) teacher's decision we abide; all the surface of the world we regard as a myrobalan in the palm of the hand.[31] All the multitude of diseases, Father, we make depart instantly, (whether) bitten by serpents, filled with poison, eaten by sickness, head sword-cloven, (or) enfeebled by Fate.' The King, hidden by a wall, hearing the whole matter, coming to the court, (and) doing obeisance like a staff[32] to the ascetic, said: 'Lord of ascetics, like unto Rudra, devoted to helping others, save me by giving life to the lad slain by me, the exceedingly

[29] Cf. IS 7400.

[30] = IS 5768.

[31] I. e., perfectly obvious.

[32] I. e., straight out flat.

sinful one.' Then said the asectic: 'King, fear not! Thy lad shall not die; by Śiva's favour he will come home. But send appurtenances for the oblation to the burning-ground together with Buddhisāgara.' Then Buddhisāgara (was) sent by the King, saying: 'Do everything as (hath been) said by the asectic.'

Then in the night Bhoja (was) secretly led there to a sandbank of the river, and the report spread (that) 'Bhoja (hath been) made alive by the ascetic.' Then Bhojarāja went to the King's palace mounted on a lordly elephant, lauded by bards, deafening the world with the noises of kettle-drums, tabors, and the like, (and) surrounded by citizens (and) ministers. And the King, embracing him, wept; but Bhoja, making Muñja cease weeping, lauded (him). Then the King, delighted, seating (Bhoja) on his own lion-throne (and) adorning (him) with the parasol and chowry, gave him the Kingdom. Giving a village to each of his own sons, he had Jayanta, the abode of (his) highest affection, live near Bhoja. Then, (his) refuge in the Other World, Muñja underwent the utmost penance, going to the forest-region of penance with his own turbaned Queens.[33] And then, by the favour of gods (and) Brāhmans, King Bhoja governed (his) Kingdom.

Thus (endeth) the Tale of Bhojarāja's Attainment of the Kingdom.

[33] Plural of majesty, as denoting the Chief Queen.

[*10*] Then, Muñja gone to the forest of penance, King Bhojarāja, appointing Buddhisāgara prime minister, enjoyed his Kingdom. Time passing thus, a Brāhman dwelling in the city of Dhārā (was) once seen by the King (as he was) going to (his) pleasure-park. And he, perceiving the King (but) closing (his) eyes (as he) went, (was) asked by the King: 'Twice-Born, (though) seeing me, thou dost not murmur "Hail!" Thou closest (thine) eyes pointedly. What (is) the cause of this?' The Brāhman said: 'Sire, thou art a Vaiṣṇavite. Thou wilt do no harm to Brāhmans; so I (have) no fear of thee. But thou givest naught to anyone; therefore thou hast no generosity. Hence, what use of benediction? Moreover, (mine) eyes (are) shut because of a proverb that "There would be loss of gain after looking on a niggard's face in the morning." And, moreover,

> 'Whose favour (is) fruitless, and wrath meaningless, him subjects desire not (as) King, even as women (desire not) a eunuch (as) husband. (47)[34]
>
> 'The knowledge of the irresolute, and the niggard's wealth, and the coward's strength of arm—these three (are) useless on earth. (48)

'Sire, my old father, going to Benares, was asked counsel by me: "Father, what ought I to do?" And thus (my) father said:

> '"If thy heart (be) wise, O sage, serve not even in a dream a King dominated by friends, dominated by eunuchs, dominated by young women. (49)
>
> '"Of all downfalls, two (are) the worst downfalls: one, a King with evil friends, and the second, dependence on him. (50)
>
> '"How (is there) a place for good folk where the King (is) of undiscriminating mind, the minister averse to the upright, and evil men (are) powerful? (51)[35]
>
> '"A King, even though bereft of good fortune, (is) to be served (as being) the refuge of qualities to be served; livelihood from him becometh fruit, even (if only) after a time." (52)

'There is no generosity whatever of a non-giver. Sire, as aforetime Lords of Earth, headed by Karṇa, Dadhīci, Śibi, (and) Vikrama,[36] (now) adorning the Other World with divine new virtues arising from their own giving, (still) dwell in earth's circuit, how about later Kings?

[34] = IS 4285.

[35] Repeated by Kālidāsa (stanza 140) as a commonplace.

[36] Karṇa was a half-brother of the Pāṇḍavas, but fought on the side of their enemies, the Kauravas, and was especially the foe of Arjuna, by whom he was killed in battle; Dadhīci was one of the Vedic sages; Śibi was so pious that he offered his whole body to save a pigeon (really Agni) from a falcon (really Indra), and later killed and prepared to eat his own son at the bidding of a Brāhman (really Viṣṇu), so pleasing the gods that his sacrifices were not required; for Vikrama see note 111.

'The body falling, what protection (is there)? Glory must be protected, (which hath) no fall; even (though his) body (be) fallen, man liveth with a body of glory. (53)

[*11*] 'Both in the sage and in the fool, in the mighty (and) in the wise, both in the lord and in the beggar, everywhere (is) equality of death. (54)

'Thy body, going on, stoppeth not even an instant; therefore, bodies (being but) transient, one should acquire glory alone. (55)

'In the midst of life is that considered by the wise (to be) the life of men which is fruitless, devoid of knowledge, courage, skill, lineage, modesty, generosity, (and) enjoyment?' (56)

As though bathed in a stream of nectar by that speech, as though merged in the Supreme Spirit, the King shed tears of joy from (his) eyes; and to the Twice-Born he said: 'Harken, most excellent Brāhman:

'In the world men (who) always say pleasing things (are) easy to get; the speaker and hearer of the unpleasant and salutary (are) hard to get. (57)[37]

'There are wise men, (but they are) not well-wishers; there are well-wishers, (but they are) not wise; one (who is) both a friend and wise (is) hard for men to get, (just) as medicine pleasant and salutary (is) hard to get.' (58)

Giving the Brāhman a lakh[38] with these words, he said: 'What (is) thy name?' The Brāhman writes on the ground his name, Govinda. The King, reading (it), said: 'Brāhman, thou must come to the palace daily; thou (hast) no denial. Sages and poets must be brought to the court of (their own) volition. Let no sage whomsoever be unhappy. Keep this (as) a governing rule.'

Some days passing thus, it became noised abroad that the King (was) a friend of sages (and) a lord of wealth for generosity. Then, eager to see the King, poets gathered together from divers quarters. Then upon a time the prime minister spoke thus to the King, (who was) spending wealth and the like: 'Sire, Kings mighty in wealth (are) victorious, not others.

'He (is) conqueror whose elephants (are) most excellent; his (is) the world; he (is) hard to attack who hath treasure; he (is) hard to conquer who hath a fortress. (59)

'Sire, regard the world:

'For the most part, it (is) precisely of the rich (that) desire for wealth (is) greatest; regard the bow, attached to the ⟨two ends of the bow⟩ (and) aiming at the ⟨mark⟩, ([for they are] attached to ⟨two crores⟩ [and] aiming at a ⟨lakh⟩ [more]).' (60)

---

[37] = IS 7131; ascribed to Yaśovarmadeva in Sūk. cx, 48; to Vikrama in Vikrama. MR xxx, 44-45.

[38] Sanskrit *lakṣa* '100,000.'

[*12*] And the King said to him:

> 'Void of giving and enjoyment, the accumulated fortune of men which is not enjoyed by friends would gradually become misfortune.' (61)[39]

With these words, the King, removing that minister from his office, put another in his office. And to him he said:

> 'A lakh should be given to a great poet, and the half thereof to a sage, and a single village to one half(-learned), the half of it to one desiring that (learning). (62)

'And among my ministers and so on, he who (is) minded to hinder giving (is) to be killed; and it (is) said:

> '"What one giveth (and) what one eateth, even that (is) the wealth of the wealthy; others sport with (his) wife and wealth (when he is) dead. (63)[40]
>
> '"Dear to folk (is) the giver, but not the (mere) lord of wealth; the water-giver [the cloud], not withholding, is beloved by the world, not the water-holder [the ocean]. (64)[41]
>
> '"The ocean, mostly intent only on accumulation, (is) in hell; behold the cloud, a giver, thundering above the earth."' (65)[42]

Thus hearing (that) Bhojarāja (was) abounding in generosity, a poet coming from the Kaliñga country[43] remained a month. And there is no sight of the Lord of Earth, and no provision for food. Then upon a time the King went out, desiring to hunt, and the poet, seeing the King, said:

> 'The mighty lord Bhojarāja seen, three things straightway fall: the sword of the foe, the poet's evil plight, (and) the knot of gazelle-eyed (women's) waist-cloths.' (66)

The King gave a lakh. Then, the King delighting in hunting, a Pulinda[44] youth sings, (and) pleased by the sweetness of (his) song, the King gave that Pulinda youth five lakhs. Then the poet, seeing that exceeding great gift and the Kirāta brat, said to the King, under the guise of a lotus lying in the lotus-hand of the Lord of Men:

> 'These qualities of thine, O lotus, though existing, attain not to manifestation, since the ⟨calix⟩ of thee, the abode of ⟨Lakṣmī⟩, is enjoyed by ⟨bees⟩

---

[39] Ascribed to Vararuci in Subhāṣ. 473.

[40] = IS 5262.

[41] = IS 4346; ascribed to Prahlādana in Sūk. cxvi, 10.

[42] Cf. IS 6676 = Mer. 140 (Taw. 84; there anonymous). The ocean was condemned to hell for grieving his mother.

[43] A district on the Coromandel Coast from below Cuttack to the vicinity of Madras.

[44] A barbarian (Mleccha) tribe or tribes; cf. the Πουλῖνδαι ἀγριοφάγοι of Ptolemy VII, i, 64, and Lassen, i, 223, note 1. Ballāla here makes the name synonymous with Kirāta, a totally different people from Eastern Nepal (Lassen, pp. 78, 530, 535, note, 1024-1025).

(since the ⟨treasury⟩ of thee, the abode of ⟨wealth⟩, is enjoyed by ⟨drunkards⟩).' (67)[45]

Bhoja, knowing that implication, again gave a lakh. Then the King said to the Brāhman:

'By Kings, O sage, art is reverenced, not family rank; (though) the gods exist, the ⟨Possessor of Digits⟩ [the moon] (and also the ⟨possessor of arts⟩) is honoured by Śambhu [Śiva] on (his) head.' (68)

[*13*] Bhoja thus speaking, five (or) six poets gathered from somewhere. Seeing them, the King was, so to say, embarrassed, thinking, 'So much money (hath been) given by me to-day!' Then the poet, knowing that implication, again said to the King, under the guise of a lotus:

'Why art thou angry at some quintessence of perfume? Be angry at thine own sweetness, for whose sake, O Thou of a Hundred Leaves [the lotus], each leaf of thee is hunted to-day by bees.' (69)[46]

Then, perceiving the King (to be of) a glad countenance, he said openly:

'A miser can neither give nor enjoy wealth; but with (his) hand he (merely) toucheth (it) like a eunuch (only touching) a woman. (70)[47]

'One would gain heaven having seen or even (simply) having heard of him who would be delighted (when) asked and glad after giving.' (71)

Then the King, pleased, again gave a lakh to the poet dwelling in the Kaliñga country. Then the first poet [Govinda], seeing the six lords of poets standing before (him), said: 'Poets, a King (is) dwelling there in the district of the bridge of the great pool; when he shall go to (his) palace, then say somewhat.' And all the great poets, knowing all the King's former wont, remained; and one of them said to the King, under the guise of a pool:

'That pool (is) best on whose road (there is) no clashing of water-jars coming empty (and) going full.' (72)

The King gave him a lakh. Then the learned Govinda, seeing those lordly poets, was angry; (and) a second poet, knowing the implication of his anger, said:

'Whose thirst dost thou not quench? Who, entering in, drinketh not thy water, unless, best of pools by a goodly road, a crocodile inhabiteth (thy) bosom?' (73)[48]

---

[45] Ascribed to Śrutadhara in Sūk. xxxii, 4.

[46] Ascribed to Śrutadhara in Sūk. xxxii, 5.

[47] = IS 3282.

[48] The 'water' and the 'pool' refer to Bhoja's generosity; the 'thirst' to the poets' desire for that generosity; the 'crocodile' to Govinda; 'the goodly road' also means 'the road of the good' (i. e., worthy recipients); anonymous in Sūk. xxxi, 2.

The King gave him [the second poet] two lakhs. And removing the learned Govinda from (his) post of office, and saying: 'Thou [second poet] must come to the court, but no one must commit iniquity,' then, giving them a lakh apiece, he went to his own city. And they went one by one.

Then upon a time the King said to the prime minister:

> 'Let him who is a fool be outside my city, even (though) a Brāhman; let him (who is) wise remain within my city, even (though) a potter.' (74)

Henceforth there was no fool whosoever in the city of Dhārā.

[*14*] Then, by degrees, five hundred sages headed by Vararuci, Bāṇa, Mayūra, Rephaṇa, Hari, Śaṅkara, Kaliṅga, Karpūra, Vināyaka, Madana, Vidyāvinoda, Kokila, (and) Tārendra,[49] versed in all sciences (and) all omniscient, adorned the court of glorious Bhojarāja. Matters standing thus, upon a time, Lord Bhoja, the crest-jewel of poets, a lover of poetry, (and) a friend dear to Brāhmans, seated on (his) lion-throne (and) lauded by a host of sages, a door-keeper coming (and) making obeisance, announced: 'Sire, a sage standeth at the door.' Then, the King commanding, 'Let him enter,' the Brāhman, brilliant with upraised right hand, said:

'O King, be there prosperity!'

The King: 'Poet Śaṅkara, what (is) this on the leaf?'

The poet: 'A verse.'

The King: 'To whom?'

The poet: 'To thee, Bhoja, Lord of Men.'

The King: 'Let it be read.'

The poet: ''Tis read:

> 'For an instant let the jingling of the bracelets on the up-tossing tendril-arms of these lotus-lovely-eyed (girls) be stayed from the quick swinging of the chowries. (75)
>
> 'Even as my heart swelleth, eager to make Bhoja's glory like the white triple earth, so is it distressed by apprehension of the whiteness of the row of curls of (his) beloved.' (76)

Then the King gave the poet Śaṅkara twelve lakhs; and all the sages became pale of face, but none spoke for fear of the King. And the King, for some reason or other, went to (his) house.

Then, seeing the court without the King, the throng of sages found fault with him: 'Oh, the ignorance of the Lord of Men! What use of serving him? He gave (only) a lakh to poets skilled in the Vedas (and)

[49] Of the poets Rephaṇa, Hari, Kaliṅga, Karpūra, Vidyāvinoda, Kokila, and Tārendra nothing further seems to be known.

śāstras (and) specialising (therein). What of him (even if) displeased? And yon Śaṅkara, merely a village-poet, what (is) his self-conceit?'

The noise of uproar arising at these words, a sage arrived, with ear-rings of gold (and) jewels, with an upper garment of beautiful cloth, like a Royal Prince with (his) limbs spotted with musk-unguent, with (his) head adorned with new flowers, [*15*] alluring with sandal cosmetic, like vivacity [50] incarnate, like poesy (that had taken) refuge in a body, with a flow (of words) like the flow of the erotic sentiment, having gained the circle of earth like great Indra. Seeing him, the assembly of sages were the recipients of fear (and) curiosity, and he, making obeisance to all, said: 'Where (is) King Bhoja?' They said to him: 'Just this moment he (hath) gone into the palace.' Then, giving them a betel apiece, he was like to a lord of beasts [a lion] gone among a herd of mighty elephants. Then the great man, learning (that) they (were) angered because of the gift to the poet Śaṅkara, said: 'Your Honours must not think twelve lakhs (have been) given to the poet Śaṅkara. The King's implication (is) not understood; the honouring of Śaṅkara being (only just) begun, the poet Śaṅkara (hath been) honoured by simply one lakh. But, knowing of the eleven Rudras in relation to him, rendered illustrious by (his) name, with forms none other than Śaṅkara's (and) visible, a lakh apiece (was) given to each of them, (and one also) to this poet Śaṅkara precisely (as having) Śaṅkara's form. (This was) the King's implication.' [51] All (were) astounded by him.

Then a servant of the King straightway announced that sage's exact words to the King. And the King, perceiving (that) that great man (had), like the Great Lord [Śiva], known his implication at once, went to the court. And he [the sage] said 'Hail' to the King. And the King, embracing (and) saluting him, clinging to his lotus-hand with his own lotus-hand, going to the palace (and) sitting in a very lofty *œil-de-boeuf*, said: 'Brāhman, what letters (are) clinging to good fortune because of Thine Honour's name? Or of what country doth Thine Honour's absence afflict the good folk?' Then the poet writes 'Kālidāsa' in the King's hand. The King, reading (this), falls at (his) feet.

Then, Kālidāsa and Bhojarāja sitting there, it was twilight, (and) the King said: 'Friend, describe the twilight.' Kālidāsa:

'The beauty of the lotus is destroyed like the knowledge of the dissolute;

---

[50] Sanskrit *vilāsa*, one of the eight manly virtues; for the 'erotic sentiment' (*śṛṅgārarasa*) as a literary style, see Regnaud, pp. 301-306.

[51] Throughout this passage there is a play on the name Śaṅkara (1) the poet who wrote the twelfth-century *bhāṇa* (monologue) *Śāradatilaka* (cf. Wilson, ii, 384-387), (2) Śiva, and (3) the eleven Rudras or Maruts, storm-gods and the friends and allies of Indra.

the bees go to wretchedness like the virtuous in a strange land; darkness oppresseth the world like an evil prince; the eye goeth to uselessness like a miser's wealth.' (77)

Again the poet praises the King:

'Service (is) to be rendered so long as men (have) no ready friends; service to those (who have) ready friends becometh deceit. (78)

[*16*] 'The whole earth, all-filled with gold, (is) given to poets by him who knoweth the glorious composition of good poetry and the way of poets. (79)[52]

'A good poet, but no other, knoweth the loveliness of diction of a good poet; verily, a barren woman knoweth not the blessing of the exceeding longings of pregnancy.' (80)

Then, step by step, friendship was born between Bhoja (and) Kālidāsa. Then, knowing Kālidāsa (to be) greedy for courtesans, all hated him; no one whosoever touches him. Then upon a time, seeing Kālidāsa in the midst of the court, Bhoja reflected: 'Wise (though he be), how hath he the intoxication of the pain of love?' Knowing his opinion, he [Kālidāsa] said:

'What is the tale of them that share the world of men in connexion with the bow-cord of the Mind-Born One [Kāma] when the virility of the Conqueror of Cities [Śiva], addicted to burning, was thus halved?' (81)[53]

Then King Bhoja, delighted, gave (him) a lakh per syllable. Then Kālidāsa praises Bhoja:

'Great King and glorious! In the world made bright by thy fame the Man Supreme [Viṣṇu] now hunteth for the Milk-Ocean; He of the Knotted Hair [Śiva] for Kailāsa; the Bearer of the Thunderbolt [Indra] for the most excellent, non-earthly elephant [Airāvata]; Rāhu for the Lord of Digits [the moon]; the Lotus-Born [Brahmā] for the *haṁsa.* (82)[54]

'Taking water (and) milk, the Lotus-Born goeth to the flocks of all birds; holding the discus, the discus-handed Mukunda [Viṣṇu] wandereth over all oceans; gazing with the eye in (his) forehead, the Lord of Cattle [Śiva] burneth all the lofty mountains; (but) the darling of thy fame (is) spread abroad in the triple world, O Prince Bhojarāja, Lord of Earth. (83)

'O Royal crest-jewel of the wise, to weigh thy glory the Creator, regarding Kailāsa, (hath) thrown there (in the balance), to fill up (its) lightness,

---

[52] Ascribed to Vallabhadeva in Sūk. iv, 18.

[53] Referring to Śiva, who burned Tripura (the 'Triple-Town' of gold, silver, and iron), and to Kāma, who inspired him with amorous passion by an arrow from his bow, but was himself consumed by the fire which burst from the god's third eye, while Śiva became androgynous (cf. stanza 241).

[54] = IS 4771. Viṣṇu directed the gods to churn the ocean to vanquish the demons; Kailāsa is the mythical mountain on which Śiva dwells; Indra rides on Airāvata, and Brahmā on the *haṁsa* (goose, gander, swan, flamingo, or other aquatic bird; sometimes—as here—merely a poetic or mythical bird); and Rāhu is the demon who swallows the moon, thus causing the eclipse.

the Bull;[55] above that, Umā's companion [Śiva]; on his head, the water of the Ganges; on its summit, the Chief of Serpents [Śeṣa]; (and) thereabove, the great Nectar-Rayed One [the moon]. (84)

'Whither, O cowherd, sage of the gods, dost thou wander from heaven on earth's surface, desirous of bringing now a pile of grass for the calf of the Wishing-Cow?[56] Fool, she (hath) no milk. [*17*] Hearing of the lavish generosity of glorious Bhojarāja, her udders (are) dry with shame. Vain were (thy) effort; all that (grass) on earth (is) devoured by his [Bhoja's] foes.' (85)

The King, delighted, gave (him) a lakh per syllable.

Then upon a time certain ones deeply versed in Revelation (and) Tradition, knowing the King (to be) fond of poetry, sat down somewhere outside the city saying: 'With the favour of Bhuvaneśvarī [Durgā] we shall make poetry.' By one among them, fancying (himself to be) a scholar, a quarter-distich was read:

'Give food,[57] O Lord of Kings.'

By another was read:

'Full of ghee (and) broth.'

The second half (of the distich) does not flash forth. Then Kālidāsa was going for worship to the temple of the goddess. Seeing him, the Brāhmans said: 'To us, though knowing all the Vedas, Bhoja giveth nothing at all, but to them like Thine Honour he giveth at pleasure. Now we (are) come here with the idea of composing poetry. Reflecting long, the first half was thought out. Making the second half, give (it us); then he offereth us something.' Having thus spoken, the half was recited before him; and he, hearing it, said:

'And a curd of buffalo-milk white (as) the moonlight of the autumnal moon.' (86)

And they, going to the King's palace, said to the door-keepers: 'We (are) come having made poetry. Show (us) the King.' And they [the door-keepers] laughing out of merriment, going (and) doing obeisance to the King, said:

'With teeth like king-beans [Dolichos Catjang] (and) hands on (their) hips, Vedist foes of *ślokas* stand at the door, O mighty King.' (87)

---

[55] The bull is the vehicle (*vāhana*) of Śiva.

[56] The Wishing-Cow (Kāmadhenu), produced at the Churning of the Ocean, is fabled to fulfil all desires, but she fails before the generosity of Bhoja, and his foes are reduced to eating grass, so that none is left for her calf. The 'sage of the gods' is Vasiṣṭha.

[57] Sanskrit *bhojana*, with an obvious allusion to the name Bhoja. The doggerel of these pedantic poetasters is so wretched that they are called enemies of true poetry. The stanza is ascribed to the Paramāra Jagaddeva in Sūk. cix, 131.

Permitted to enter by the King, seeing the King's assembly, (and) grouping themselves, they recited the poem together. The King, hearing it (and) knowing the latter half (to have been) made by Kālidāsa, said to the Brāhmans: 'Never should poetry be made from the mouth of him by whom the first half (was) caused to be made. Something is given for the latter half, not for the first half.' With these words he gave a lakh per syllable. And they gone with their largess, the King said, looking at Kālidāsa: 'Poet, the latter half (was) made by thee.' The poet said:

> 'The sweetness of a (woman's) lip, the firmness of (her) breasts, and the keenness of (her) eyes, (and) ripeness in poetry (only) he distinguisheth (who hath) the taste of experience.' (88)

And the King: 'Good poet, thou sayest sooth:

> [*18*] 'Unprecedented shineth the flavour of speech in the immortal fruit of poetry; the taste being else all equal, only the poet knoweth (its) sweetness. (89)

> 'Reflecting, reflecting on the world (as) a whole, three things enter the heart: the products of the sugar-cane, the minds of poets, (and) the fleeting, side-long glances of bashful (women).' (90)[58]

Then upon a time a door-keeper, making obeisance, said to Bhoja: 'O King, a poet from the Drāviḍa country, named Lakṣmīdhara, sitteth at the door.' The King said: 'Let him enter.' Seeing him (when he had) entered shining like the sun, (and also seeing that) he (had) long (been) ignorant of events, the King reflected and said:

> 'Happy they—wishes fulfilled by discerning merely (external) appearance—who nowhere hear the wretched songs of beggars.' (91)[59]

And he [Lakṣmīdhara], coming there, saying 'Hail,' (and) seated at his [Bhoja's] command, said: 'Sire, this thy court (is) adorned by scholars, and thou art Viṣṇu in bodily form. What, then, (is) my learning? So I say somewhat:

> '(All) else rejected by the Creator in creating Bhoja's splendour, what need of infinitesimal atoms? The bolt was he in Hari's hand, and the sun in the sky, the fire in the ocean.' (92)[60]

Then the assembly (were) amazed by him, and the King gave him a lakh per syllable. Again said the poet: 'Sire, I have come here together with (my) household with the hope of dwelling (in Dhārā).

> 'By merit a master patient, generous, (and) appreciative of quality is gained; a poet agreeable, honest, clever, (and) wise (is) right hard to gain.' (93)[61]

---

[58] For the 'bashful' heroine (*mugdhā*) see Schmidt, pp. 260-263.

[59] Śārṅ. 268 = IS 847.

[60] See note 127.

[61] Cf. IS 2013.

Then said the King to the prime minister: 'Let a house be given to this poet.' Then the prime minister, examining the whole city, saw no fool by whose eviction a house is given to the sage. Then roving everywhere (and) perceiving the house of a certain weaver, he said to the weaver: 'Weaver, go out from (thy) house; a sage will come to thy house.' Then the weaver, going to the King's palace (and) doing obeisance to the King, said: 'Sire, Thy Majesty's minister, making me out a fool, expelleth (me) from (my) house. But see thou (whether I am) a fool or a scholar.

'(If) I make (mere) poetry, I do not make (it) particularly pleasing; if I make (it) carefully, I do make (it) particularly pleasing. [*19*] O thou characterised by daring, (whose) footstool (is) adorned with the crest-jewels of Kings, I make poetry, I weave, I go.' (94)

Then the King said to the weaver speaking with utterance of the word 'thou':[62] 'Delightful (is) thy series of words, and beautiful the sweetness of (thy) poetry; but poetry should be spoken after reflection.' Then the weaver, angered, said: 'Sire, the answer here is obvious, but I do not say (it); the duty of Kings (is) different to the duty of the wise.' The King said: 'If there is an answer, speak.' The weaver said: 'Sire, I consider no one a poet except Kālidāsa. Save Kālidāsa, who in thy court is a sage knowing the true (nature) of poetry?

'The might of eloquence arising from the ripeness of the nectar of the teacher's compassion (is) to be taken by the poet, not by violence to (them that) enjoy fame for study. What perfume of a mass of lotuses doth a buffalo get, though dwelling (all) day in a pond, but (only) making the water-flood muddy? (95)

'This my word-weaving, sweet with the skill of splendid quarter-verses (and) with brilliant combinations, (is) barren in the heart of others (than poets, but) successful in a poet's heart; the side-long glance of a lovely-eyed (woman), falling from the corner of a slightly-opened eye (is) vain in (the case of) a child, but somewhat delighteth young men.' (96)

Sītā, lauded by wise folk, said:

'A fool is distressed at poetry to be essayed (only) by the great-hearted, not at his own folly; a woman (whose) breasts (are) dry usually blameth (her) bodice.' (97)[63]

Then said the weaver:

'In the childhood of sons, in intercourse with women, in the praise of poets, (and) in the battle of warriors addresses conjoined with "thou" (are) lauded; remember *thou*, O King, what (is) *thy* burden of folly!' (98)

---

[62] He had disrespectfully used the second person singular (*tvam* and *paśya*), unfitting in addressing one of exalted station (cf. Manu xi, 205, and stanza 98, where the weaver reproaches Bhoja for ignoring this rule).

[63] Ascribed to Arghaṭa in Sūk. iv, 19, and Subhāṣ. 153.

Then the King, saying: 'Bravo, noble weaver!' gave him a lakh per syllable, (and) again he said to the weaver: 'Fear not!'

Some time having thus gradually elapsed, the most excellent scholar Bāṇa, highly esteemed by the King, experiences poverty in consequence of former *karma*. Under these circumstances, upon a time the King, roving about in his city alone (and) disguised, coming to Bāṇa's house, stood there. [*20*] Then at midnight Bāṇa, because of distraction from poverty, said to (his) beloved: 'Lady, how often did the King fulfil my wish! Even to-day he giveth again (if) asked; but a fool's tongue itself becometh dull in the taste of continual asking.' So speaking, he remained silent half a *muhūrta* [twenty-four minutes]. Again he recites:

> 'O Seizer, Seizer, Seizer of Cities! Where (is) the hardness of (distinguishing between) the words "poison"[64] (and) "vain asking?" Only thy taste-knower [tongue] (is) cognisant of the difference in taste between them both. (99)

'Lady,

> 'The uttermost form of poverty (is) begging, not paucity of wealth; though possessed (only) of a loin-cloth, Śambhu [Śiva] (is) yet the Supreme Lord. (100)

> 'Subservience to comforts, wasting of wealth, begging from the great, an evil prince of subjects, a son of ruined character, (and) a blow at the root of families—(each of these is) a hard ax. (101)

'So, (my) poverty existing, I myself cannot speak to the King.

> 'The cloud, though giving (only) for an instant, gaineth the affection of all the world; the sun, constantly sending forth (his) rays, createth burning. (102)[65]

'And moreover, Lady, (the proverb,) "They (who have) come at the time of the All-God rite[66] afterward go away hungry"—that burneth my heart.

> 'The burning of the fire of poverty (is) quenched by the water of gratification; by what is the inward fire of a beggar's stricken hope quenched?' (103)[67]

---

[64] For Śiva at (Tri)pura see note 53; the poison *halāhala* was produced at the Churning of the Ocean and was drunk by Śiva to save the world, whence his name Nīlakaṇṭha ('Blue-Neck').

[65] Cf. IS 5021.

[66] A rite in which food is offered to the ancestors.

[67] = stanza 282 (there spoken by Māgha, as in Mer. 87 [Taw. 51] and Śārṅ. 406); ascribed to Bhaṭṭapradyumna in Subhāṣ. 504.

And the King, hearing all that, departed, saying: 'He should not be given anything now; to-morrow I shall fulfil Bāṇa's wish.

> 'What use of poems, powers, (or) riches by which (one is) not made eloquent, and by which the unfortunate attaineth not to protection, (and) by which a petitioner (is) not as one's self?' (104)

The King thus roving about in the city, comes, in (his) course, upon two thieves. One of them, Śakunta, said: 'Friend, though the world (have) thick darkness diffused (throughout it), by means of an unguent I see wealth everywhere even if well-nigh infinitesimal atoms; but even a mass of gold brought from a store-house (is) of no profit to me.' The second thief, named Marāla, said: 'Why (dost thou) say that even a mass of gold fetched from a store-house (is) not good?' Then said Śakunta: 'City-guards are roving about everywhere; [*21*] everyone will be awake through the noise of their kettle-drums, tabors, and the like. Therefore, dividing (what hath been) brought, and each taking the wealth falling to his share, we must go quickly.' Marāla said: 'Friend, what wilt thou do with this mass of jewels (and) gold estimated at two crores?'

Śakunta: 'I shall give this wealth to some Brāhman so that he, thoroughly knowing the Vedas and Vedāṅgas [texts ancillary to the Vedas], asketh of no other man.'

Marāla: 'Dear friend,

> 'If (there be) horripilation both of self and of others giving, battling, (or) reading, that gift (is) traditionally manly. (105)

'How will the fruit of merit be thine by that gift?'

Śakunta: 'This (is) the prescribed duty [*dharma*] of our father (and) grandfather that wealth is acquired by theft.'

Marāla: 'Admitting decapitation (as the punishment for theft), how is all (that) wealth, (once) acquired, given?

Śakunta:

> 'A fool giveth not wealth through fear of poverty; a wise man bestoweth wealth through fear of poverty.' (106)

Marāla:

> 'A certain vessel [worthy person] (is) composed of Veda; a certain vessel (is) composed of penance; the highest of vessels (is) the vessel in whose belly (is) no *śūdra*-food.' (107)

Śakunta: 'What will Thine Honour do with that wealth?'

Marāla: 'Friend, a Brāhman stripling dwelling in Benares came here.

By him the fruit of dwelling in Benares (was) described before our father. Then our dad, practising theft from youth, (but) by Divine will turning from sin, will go to Benares with (his) family. For his sake (is) this mass of wealth.'

Śakunta: 'Great luck for thy father! For thus—

> 'Doth the wretched conqueror of Pāka [68] become equal to a dog (whose) soul (is) perfumed by the desire of dwelling in the city of Benares? (108)
>
> 'A salt-impregnated field of the crops of *karma* [69] (is) the city of Benares, where Release is gained alike by Caṇḍālas [outcastes] and by scholars. (109)
>
> 'Where death (is) bliss, and ashes adornment, where a loin-cloth (is) a silken robe—that (is) Benares. With what is it measured?' (110)

[*22*] Thus hearing the conversation of (them) both, the King rejoiced, and in (his) mind he thought: 'Everywhere the course of deeds (is) manifold; the mind of both (is) pure.'

Then the King, returning within the palace, saw a father (and) son. There the father said to the son: 'Now the Prince, though knowing the truth of the *śāstras,* through niggardliness giveth nothing at all. Moreover,

> 'A petitioner composing poetry, *he* [the King] composeth poetry; (a petitioner) reciting, *he* reciteth; (a petitioner being on the) point of lauding, *he* laudeth; (a petitioner) saying, "I go," *he,* silent, shutteth (his) eyes.' (111)

Hearing this, going to him, saying: 'Speak not so,' taking all the adornments from his limbs, (and) giving (them) to him, then going to the palace, (and) entering the court after a while, the King said to Kālidāsa: 'Friend,

> 'I praise the mind of poets; they swim in the Water of Mind.'

Kālidāsa said:

> 'Where, like *haṁsa*-birds, are the worlds fourteen.' (112) [70]

Then the King gave (him) a lakh of pearls per syllable. Then a door-keeper enters, saying: 'Sire, a sage with (only) a loin-cloth left standeth at the door.' The King: 'Let him enter.' Then the poet,

[68] One of the demons by killing whom Indra became lord of the gods.

[69] I. e., the results of *karma* (deeds done in a former incarnation) are destroyed, so that highest and lowest alike obtain release from transmigration.

[70] Ascribed to Rājaśekhara in Sūk. iv, 3; there are seven heavens above and seven below; the 'Water of Mind' (*Pratibhāmbhas*) is a synonym of Mānasa, a lake on Mount Kailāsa, where Śiva and Kubera have their paradise; for the *haṁsa* see note 54 and Hopkins, p. 19.

permitted to enter, approaching, uttering the word 'Hail,' (and) seating himself without even being spoken to, said:

> 'Here[71] dwelleth Meru, the crest of mountains, and here, in sooth, (are) the seven seas with (their) burdens laid down; this earth, unequalled (and) unending, fit for supporting the production of many beings, (is) the place of (them that possess) our rule.' (113)

The King: 'Great poet, tell (us) what (is) thy name.'

The poet: 'Asking the name of scholars (is) not customary. Even so, we speak (it) if thou knowest (how to deduce it).

> 'Suckling wisdom by no means plungeth into a deep saying; a bamboo staff is not (able) to see the ocean's bottom. (114)

'Harken, Sire:

> 'May the Moon-Dweller [Śiva], to whom the Mountain's Daughter [Pārvatī] of laughing countenance said, "Look," making into a circle a fallen digit of the moon and a bracelet broken in amorous combat, [*23*] give protection, and the Mountain-Born (herself), and the Play-Moon [*krīḍācandra*], (his) body filled with rays of teeth.' (115)[72]

Kālidāsa: 'Friend Krīḍācandra, thou art seen at last! How (is) thy plight thus, (when) every region (is) radiant, and the King abundantly rich?'

Krīḍācandra:

> 'Even though rich, (they whose) wealth (consisteth) in non-giving are reckoned (as) in the forefront of the very poor; since it killeth not thirst, therefore (is) the ocean itself merely a desert.' (116)

'And, moreover:

> 'The wealth of men timid in enjoyment (of it), whose chief object (is) accumulation of money, abideth at home, like a jewel of a maiden, for another's sake. (117)
>
> 'By gold, jewels, bracelets, (and) drums other lords of earth (gain place); simply by artistry, O Bhoja, one knowing (true) values gaineth their place. (118)
>
> 'Composed of nectar, so to speak, poems distil nectar (though) without clever composition, just as the youth of courtesans (is) charming in (its) guilelessness. (119)
>
> 'Even the name of a king is not known without poetry; without him [the King] the poet's fame shineth not on earth.' (120)

---

[71] I. e., at Bhoja's court.

[72] Also ascribed to Krīḍācandra in Śārṅ. 96, but to Vararuci in Sad. I, xi, 5, and to Candaka in Subhāṣ. 66.

Mayūra:

'They (are) praiseworthy, they (are) great of soul, their glory (is) steadfast in the world by whom poems (are) composed and who (are) glorified in poetry.' (121)

Vararuci:

'In this the poets' way, charming through union with the wise (because) manifestly made manifest by verses, shineth the thought of (one who is) merely wise; and this path of sidelong glances of virtuous ladies, betraying attachment to a bit of play, in sooth, (is) not impossible for courtesans.' (122)[73]

The King gave Krīḍācandra twenty lordly elephants and five villages. Then the poet praises the King:

'Bracelet on the eyes, sect-mark on the finger—Oh, the strangeness of the adornments of the wives of Bhoja's foes!' (123)

[*24*] The King, pleased, again gave (him) a lakh per syllable.

Then upon a time a sage named Rāmeśvara, all (his) limbs out-worn by age, came to the court and said:

'For a lion (and) a good poet, by elephant-meat (for the one and) the King's grace (for the other), breaking of the fast is found somewhere for the faster everywhere. (124)

'Of beasts of burden and of scholars some one (is) supreme over others; of lords of poets (and) of lords of elephants the highest recipient (is) the King. (125)

'Even so:

'With golden (ornaments) and silken garments would be the splendour of courtesans; with valour (and) generosity shine the sons of Kings.' (126)

Hearing this, the King, taking off (all) his adornments, gave two lakhs to the scholar Rāmeśvara. Then the poet praises (him):

'Bhoja, the great musk-mark of thy darling Fame shineth set on heaven's brow, O King, mine of virtues! (127)

'Before the wise one should not tell (one's) virtues, for he himself well knoweth (them); before the fool he should not tell (them; the fool) knoweth not (what is) said by the wise.' (128)

All (were) astounded at him. The poet Rāmeśvara:

'The good man maketh fame to come, the good poet simply maketh poetry; water maketh the lotus grow, but the sun maketh (it) conjoined with beauty.' (129)[74]

---

[73] Ascribed to Harihara in Sūk. iv, 35.

[74] Ascribed to Ravigupta in Subhāṣ. 154.

Then the King, delighted, gave (him) a lakh per syllable. The poet said to the Lord of Kings:

> 'A niggard, abandoned by fame, doth not even hear poetry; what doth a eunuch do with a gazelle-eyed one standing before him?' (130)

Sītā said:

> 'Poets stricken by Fate, piteous they, (and) elephants too; no splendour becometh theirs without the house of a Lord of the Land.' (131)

Kālidāsa:

> 'Nowhere do a poet's songs touch a non-giver's mind; to the distress of the exceeding old sports are made young.' (132)

[*25*] The King gave a lakh per syllable.

Then upon a time, seeing Kālidāsa approaching, superior to the poet-circle combined, the King was yet a little grieved in mind because of (Kālidāsa's) greed for courtesans. Then Sītā, lauded by the host of the wise, knowing his (Bhoja's) opinion, said: 'Sire,

> 'Even (though) seeing a fault in a virtuous man, lovers of virtue are not distressed; with affection indeed doth the world behold a spot fallen in the moon.' (133)[75]

The King, delighted, gave a lakh to Sītā. When, even so, he does not esteem Kālidāsa as aforetime, then Kālidāsa, also knowing the King's opinion, said, under the guise of a lotus:

> 'Attained to the way of a standard, what, O balance, in sooth (is) thy pride? Thou bringest the weightiest low, and puttest its opposite higher.' (134)

Again he said:

> 'Why doth he whose way is everywhere go to sorrow through love for his own land? What men drink brackish water saying: "This (is) daddy's well?"' (135)[76]

Then, knowing in (his) mind the contempt formed by the King, Kālidāsa went sadly to his own house.

> Affection burst by contempt, who (is) the lord to make (it) the same (as it was aforetime)? A burst pearl is not joined by smearing (it) with lac. (136)[77]

Then the King, too, was dejected. Then Līlāvatī,[78] seeing the King

[75] Ascribed to Ravigupta in Subhāṣ. 244.

[76] Cf. IS 5415.

[77] This stanza and 184, 319, and 321 are the only ones in the entire work not ascribed to some individual.

[78] Līlā(vatī) was Bhoja's Chief Queen.

dejected, asked the reason for (his) sadness; and the King told her all privately. And she, knowing (his) contempt for Kālidāsa from the King's mouth, again said: 'Sire, master of (my) life, thou art omniscient.

> 'Affection not formed (is) best; affection born (but afterward) broken (is) not best; he (whose) eyes (are) destroyed indeed (is) sad; not sad is he (who is) blind from birth. (137)

'But Kālidāsa (is) some human incarnation of Bhāratī [Sarasvatī]. Therefore honour him with all (thy) might with (the other) sages. Behold:

> 'Even (though) a 〈mine of faults〉 and 〈causing darkness〉, even (though) crooked, even (though) spotted, even (though) with rising ordained at the time of the setting of the sun, [*26*] yet the moon attaineth to the affection of Hara [Śiva]; there should be no distinction of virtues (and) vices in them (that have) sought refuge.' (138)

Acknowledging that 'All this (is) true, dear,' the King said: 'To-morrow morning I shall make Kālidāsa content.'

The next day the King, performing the rite of cleansing (his) teeth and so forth, (but) omitting (other) obligatory duties, went to the court. Scholars and poets, singers and other subjects all assembled. The King, seeing (that) Kālidāsa alone (had) not come, sent his own servant alone to the courtesan's house to summon him. And he, going (and) making obeisance to Kālidāsa, said: 'Lord of poets, Bhoja, Lord of Men, summoneth thee.' Then the poet reflected: 'Yesterday I (was) despised by the King; what (is) the reason for the summons early to-day?

> 'A King's friends strive for the expulsion of whomsoever the King honoureth in the assembly. (139)

'But I daily being especially honoured by the King, tricksters, through envy, rouse up hostility (against me).

> 'How (is there) a place for good folk where the King (is) of undiscriminating mind, the minister averse to the upright, and evil men (are) powerful?' (140)[79]

So reflecting, he went to the court. Then, seeing (him) coming afar off, arising joyfully from (his) seat, (and) saying: 'Good poet dearest to me, why is delay made to-day?' (the King) goes five (or) six steps toward (Kālidāsa). Then all the court rose from their seats, and all the courtiers (were) astounded, and his enemies became pale. Then the King, taking (his) lotus-hand with his own lotus-hand, going to his

[79] = stanza 51 (there spoken by an aged Brāhman).

own seat, and making him sit on the lion-throne, himself sat right there at his bidding. Then, Kālidāsa mounted on the King's lion-throne, the poet Bāṇa, raising (his) right arm, said:

> 'From honouring ⟨Kālidāsa⟩, the ⟨servant of Kālī [80]⟩, Bhoja, ⟨knowing the (sixty-four) arts⟩, by whom he (Kālidāsa), though a ⟨mine of faults⟩, (is) made King ⟨among the very wise⟩, (is) like Rudra, ⟨finding the (sixteen) digits (of the moon)⟩ from honouring the ⟨servant of the dark cloud-mass (the moon)⟩, by whom he (the moon), though the ⟨maker of darkness⟩, (is) made King ⟨among the gods⟩.' (141)

Then the fire of enmity with the sages (was) especially kindled against him.

Then by all the sages, taking counsel with certain wise men, a slave-girl, Bhoja's betel-bearer, [*27*] (was) honoured with money, gold, and the like. And craftily they said to her: 'Beautiful one, this Kālidāsa draineth our renown. Who among us doth not show equality of art with him? Thy Loveliness must act so, dear, that the King expel him to another land.' The slave-girl said: 'Receiving a pearl-necklace from Your Honours, what should be done for you by me is done. So the necklace must be given to me first.' Then the betel-bearer, taking the necklace given by them, reflected: 'What is not to be accomplished by the wise?'

Then, some days having elapsed, the King, by Fate, fell asleep alone; (and she) having performed the service of massaging his feet and so on, slept right there, closing (her) eyes deceitfully. Then, correctly knowing, by the movement of (his) feet, (that) the King (was) a little wakeful, she said: 'Friend Madanamālinī, that evil-souled Kālidāsa, gaining the women's apartments by a slave-girl's dress, disporteth himself with Queen Līlā.' Hearing that, the King, rising up, said: 'Taraṅgavatī, art thou awake?' And she, as if filled with sleep, hears not. And the King, hearing her ill sound, reflected: 'In slumber this Taraṅgavatī, under sleep's dominion, by force of memory telleth the Queen's misconduct; and it (is) indeed possible that he cometh to the harem with female dress. Who, in sooth, knoweth women's way?'

And then, thus reflecting, early on the morrow, feigning a fever, lying down, having Kālidāsa brought by a slave-girl, and, immediately after his coming, having Queen Līlā brought by that (same girl), the King addressed the Queen: 'Dear, I must take medicine right now.' This said, she (answering), 'Quite so,' getting the medicine (and) giving

[80] Kālī (Durgā) is the wife of Rudra (Śiva). For the shortening of the final *ī* in composition cf. Pāṇini VI, iii, 63.

(it) to the King in a silver bowl, prepared bean-broth there. Then the King, wishing to know the intent of them both, spoke a half-verse:

> 'How, O lord of poets, (is) bean-broth, evil for disease, huskless?'

Then Kālidāsa, the Queen close by, spoke the other half:

> 'In union with ⟨water (and) a supervisor [cook]⟩ (its) ⟨husk⟩ (is) gone (⟨blind one⟩, in union with ⟨(her) lover⟩ (her) ⟨bodice⟩ [is] gone).' (142)

Hearing that, the Queen, with knowledge of the true nature of the matter (and), like Sarasvatī, knowing its character, smiled a little. The King, seeing that, reflected: 'She loveth Kālidāsa of old; thus it hath been told by him in her presence, and she hath smiled. Who knoweth women's way? [81]

> [28] 'The bound of a horse and Indra's roar [thunder] and the mind of women, the fate of man, both lack of rain and excess of rain God knoweth not; how should man? (143) [82]

'However, this Brāhman must not be killed (even) in (his) horrible guilt, especially (as being) a human incarnation of Sarasvatī.' Reflecting thus, he said to Kālidāsa: 'Poet, under no circumstances mayest (thou) remain in our land. What (is the use) of much speaking? No reply whatever may be uttered.' Then Kālidāsa, rising agitatedly (and) going to the courtesan's house, said to her: 'Dear, give permission (for me to depart).[83] Bhoja, angry at me, hath said that (I) may not remain in his land. Alas!

> 'It joineth a joining of the unjoined; joinings of the well-joined it maketh hard to join—Fate, indeed, joineth those (things) which man thinketh (are) not (joinable). (144) [84]

'Moreover, it is evident that something (hath been) set on foot by a group of sages; for thus:

> 'A combination of many (things) of little strength (is) hard to overcome; with dry grasses is made a rope whereby elephants are bound.' (145) [85]

Then the courtesan, named Vilāsavatī, said to him:

> 'He, indeed, (is) one's best friend in whom two things combine: both weal and woe seen like a reflection in a mirror. (146)

---

[81] In his jealousy, Bhoja takes the bad sense in Kālidāsa's punning line, which may also mean: 'In union with (her) ⟨lover in the dark⟩ (her) ⟨bodice⟩ (is) gone.'

[82] = IS 729; to Bhartṛhari in Vikrama. SR ii, 9; JR ii, 12.

[83] Indian courtesy requires a host to give his guest permission to depart.

[84] = IS 79; to Dhanada in Vikrama. JR vii, 3.

[85] Cf. IS 4425; to Vyāsa in Sūk. cx, 9.

'Darling, (if) I (am) known, what (hast) thou (to do) with the King, or what (hast thou) to do with wealth given by the King? Stay comfortably (and) securely in the inner cellar of my house.' Then Kālidāsa passed several days dwelling there.

Then, Kālidāsa gone from the house, Queen Līlā said to the King: 'Sire, (thy) very closest friendship (was) with the poet Kālidāsa. Why, now, this extraordinary action wherefore dwelling in the land (is) forbidden?

> 'As from the sugar-cane's tip superiority of sap (increaseth) node by node, so (is) the friendship of good folk; (but) of the reverse, the reverse. (147)[86]

> 'A protection against grief (and) foe, a recipient of affection (and) trust, by whom (was) this jewel, the disyllable "friendship," created?' (148)[87]

[*29*] The King, hearing that utterance of Queen Līlā, said: 'Lady, by some one it hath been told me that "Kālidāsa, reaching the women's apartments by a slave-girl's dress, disporteth himself with the Queen." And through a feigned fever he and Thy Ladyship (were) observed by me with a desire to know that matter. Then, thou thyself present, he said the second half[88] thus. Hearing that, thou didst laugh. And then he (hath been) expelled from the land by me, seeing all that, (but) fearing the killing of a Brāhman; and through kindness thee I kill not.' Then the Queen, filled with laughter,[89] astonished, said: 'Surely, Sire, rich indeed (am) I, of whom thou (art) such an husband. How doth the mind of me, accustomed to enjoyment just with thee, go elsewhere, since thou art to be remembered by all loving women in enjoyment with (their) lovers? Alas, Sire, if thou shalt go without having proved me faithful or unfaithful, then in any case I shall die.' Then the King: 'Dear, thou sayest sooth.' Then the Prince had a serpent brought by (his) men; he had a hot iron ball made; and made ready a bow. Then the Queen, having bathed, blazing intensely with the fire of devotion to her own husband, (and) with very tender limbs, said, looking at the sun: 'Eye of the world, thou, seeing all, knowest all.

> 'In waking and in time of dream, (or) in deep slumber, if my husband Bhoja only, and not another, (is) in my mind, thou art not thought about.' (149)[90]

---

[86] = IS 1088; anonymous in Sūk. cxx, 8.

[87] = IS 6527.

[88] Of stanza 142.

[89] At Bhoja's absurd and groundless suspicion.

[90] I. e., she need not fear the sun's judgement, for she will be proved innocent in the ordeal.

So speaking, she then performed the triple ordeal. Then, the pure Līlāvatī in the harem, the King, his head bowed in shame (and) sick with repentance,[91] said: 'Lady, forgive me, most evil! What (can) I say?' And thenceforth the King sleeps not and eats not, talks with none; (his) mind simply shuddering, he wails day (and) night: 'What (is) my shame; what (my) consideration; where (my) depth (of character)? Oh, Oh, poet, topmost crest-jewel of poets, Kālidāsa! Oh, (thou) like (mine own) life! By a fool thou (hast been) made to hear a thing not to be heard! Thou hast been spoken to unspeakably!' As if asleep, as if devoured by a Seizer,[92] as if darkened by Delusion, he fell (to the ground). Then, consciousness restored by water sprinkled by the lotus-hand of (his) beloved, scarcely seeing that same beloved (and) filled with self-reproach, he finally stood (up). Then, like night deprived of the lord of night [the moon], like the beauty of day deprived of the maker of day [the sun], like a young woman separated (from her darling), like the assembly-hall of the gods forsaken by Indra, the court of King Bhoja, forsaken by Kālidāsa, shines not. Thenceforth (there is) no poesy in the mouth of any; no one speaks a word lovely for enjoyment.

[*30*] Then upon a time, some days having passed, beholding the circle of the full moon in Rākā,[93] and regarding the moon-face of Queen Līlā before (him), he [Bhoja] said:

> 'Atom-like yon lunar orb pursueth after equality with the moon-face of this (lady).

'And where, even at full moon, (are) the delights of the eyes? Where the pastime of speech?' And rising in the morning, performing the morning rites, and reaching the court, the King said to the most excellent sages: 'Poets, let this *samasyā*[94] be completed.' Then he recites:

> 'Atom-like yon lunar orb pursueth after equality with the moon-face of this (lady).'

Again he said: 'If this *samasyā* is not completed by Your Honours, there can be no abiding in my land.' Then the poets, affrighted, went to their homes. Even (though) the meaning (is) pondered long, conjunction with the meaning flashes forth to no one. Then Bāṇa,

[91] Reading *paścāttāpāturaḥ* with V and T instead of *paścāttāpātpuraḥ* with P.

[92] See note 19.

[93] The goddess presiding over the full moon.

[94] *Samasyā* is a portion of a stanza given to another person for completion (cf. p. 7).

joining with (them) all, (was) sent. Then, reaching the court, he said to the King: 'Sire, I (am) sent by all the sages. Grant an extension for eight days; on the ninth day they will complete (the *samasyā*) for thee; otherwise, they go out from (thy) land.' Then said the King: 'Very well.' Then Bāṇa, informing them of the King's message, went to his house. Then eight days passed. The poets being assembled on the night of the eighth day, Bāṇa said: 'Alas! Through intoxication of youth, through intoxication of the King's esteem, through intoxication of some (small) knowledge, Kālidāsa was expelled. All Your Honours (are) equal poets; but on a different plane he alone (is) a poet. Expelling him, what greatness is there now? If he (were) here, how would your plight be this? What wisdom (was) shown in his expulsion is perceived by Your Honours yourselves.

> 'In hatred of Brāhmans there would surely be destruction of (one's own) race; but in hatred of a form of Umā,[95] destruction of the race of poets.' (150)

Then all, Mayūra[96] and the rest, quarrelled violently. Then they, immediately ceasing all quarrels, said: 'The extension is fulfilled to-day; excepting Kālidāsa, no one hath ability to complete the *samasyā*.

> 'In the conflict of mighty warriors, in the poet-circle of poets, in an instant is born either glory or the loss of glory. (151)

'If it please (you), then this very day, the moon set at midnight, we go secretly with the abundance of (our) acquisitions. If we go not, to-morrow the King's servants expel us [*31*] by force; then we must go with (our) bodies only. So we shall go to-day at midnight.' Thus reflecting, going home, and mounting the abundance of (their) wealth on ox-drawn carts, all set forth at night. Then Kālidāsa, staying right there at night in the garden of Vilāsavatī's house, (and) hearing their voice (as they were) coming along the road, sent a maid-servant of the courtesan, saying: 'Dear, see who are these coming like Brāhmans.' Then she, approaching, saw them all; and returning, said to Kālidāsa:

> 'There was not that beauty of the lake with a thousand cranes dwelling round about its shores that (there was) with a single royal swan. (152)

'And all, Bāṇa, Mayūra, and the rest, are fleeing; (there is) no doubt of it.' Kālidāsa: 'Quickly bring (my) clothes from the house, dear, that I may protect the fleeing poets.

[95] I. e., Kālidāsa, since Umā is a synonym for Kālī; Kālidāsa was both a poet and, according to tradition, a Brāhman by birth.

[96] On Mayūra in the *Bhojaprabandha* see G. P. Quackenbos, *The Sanskrit Poems of Mayūra*, New York, 1917, pp. 43-48.

'What (were) the heroism (of him) who protecteth not the afflicted, or what the wealth that were not for needy folk; what that action that (were) not connected with weal; what the life that (were) hostile to the good?' (153)

Then Kālidāsa, donning a bard's costume, carrying a sword, going half a *kos*[97] farther, coming face to face with them, surveying (them) all, (and) uttering the benediction 'Conquer!' asked, with the voice of a bard: 'Oceans of Wisdom, attained to pre-eminence of greatness at Bhoja's court, (and) together like Bṛhaspatis,[98] whither (are) Your Honours desirous of going? How (is) your health? And (is) the King well? We are going from the land of Benares to see Bhoja and with hope of wealth.' Then all departed, deriding (him).

Then a poet among them, hearing his speech and deeming him a bard, eagerly said: 'Listen, bard! Thou wilt hear (it) later, so I tell thee right now. A *samasyā* (hath been) spoken by the King for completion by these sages. Unable to complete it, these have set out desiring to go somewhere in another land from fear of the angered King.' The bard: 'What *samasyā* (was) spoken by the King?' Then the poet recites:

'Atom-like yon lunar orb pursueth after equality with the moon-face of this (lady).'

The bard: 'That (hath its) meaning well hidden indeed; this was recited by the King seeing the circle of the full moon; the second half of it ought to be this:

[*32*] '"Atom-like" describeth to some degree an imitation of that moon's beginning.'

All, hearing (this, were) astounded. Then the bard, making obeisance to all, departed. Then all reflected: 'Oh, this (is) plainly Sarasvatī, come in human form for the saving of us all; this cannot be a man. Even now nothing is known by any one. So, quickly going home (and) taking the load from the carts, to-morrow (we) must all go to the King's palace; otherwise the bard will make (the completion of the *samasyā*) known. So we go at once.' Yoking up, they did so. Then going to the King's court, seeing the King, (and) saying 'Hail,' they entered. Then said Bāṇa: 'Sire, the Lord only knoweth what is recited by thee, the omniscient. Who (are) these wretched gluttonous Brāhmans? Thus is it said:

[97] The *kos* (Sanskrit *krośa* 'shout') varies greatly in length in different localities, but is usually between one-and-a-half and two miles (cf. Yule-Burnell, pp. 261-262).

[98] In later Hinduism, the deity of wisdom and eloquence.

'Atom-like yon lunar orb pursueth after equality with the moon-face of this (lady); "atom-like" describeth to some degree an imitation of that moon's beginning.' (154)[99]

The King, knowing the implication (of that) as determined (by him), said: 'In any case Kālidāsa dwelleth in a place to be reached in a day; and everything can be accomplished by strategems.' Then he gave Bāṇa fifteen lakhs of gold pieces. As if under pretext of (the King's) contentment, the group of sages (were) sent each to his own house.

And, the circle of sages quietly gone, the King commanded a door-keeper: 'If any twice-born shall come, then they must be brought into the house.' Then, Bāṇa gone to his house with all the wealth, certain scholars said: 'Oh, an irregular thing was done by Bāṇa, since he, though going out from the city with us, (hath) taken all the wealth. By all means we shall let Bhoja know Bāṇa's real character that no one whosoever may commit impropriety among sages.' Then they, going to the King, saw (him). The King said to them: 'The real character of this (matter[100] is) known. Your Honours must speak truthfully.' Then all (was) made known by them.

Then the King reflected: 'In any case Kālidāsa, for fear of me, dwelleth in my city in a bard's costume.' And then he commanded (his) body-guards: 'Ho! let horses be saddled.'[101] Then, in the departure from the pleasure-garden, the sound of drums arose. 'Oh, now we have heard that the King (is) engrossed [*33*] in worshipping the gods; now again he will go to the pleasure-garden.' All the soldiers, bewildered, go behind together. Then the King, mounting (his) horse, came with the sages to the place where the incident of the bard took place at night. Then the King, summoning (men) skilled in tracking the foot-prints of roving thieves, said: 'The foot-prints of whomsoever (hath) gone out by this road at night are seen to-day; let them be looked at.'

Then, giving a lakh to each scholar and dismissing them, the King went to his own house. And the trackers, going everywhere at the King's command, (but) not seeing (the man they sought), were, so to speak, perplexed. And then at setting sun, seeing a slave-girl going to a leather-worker's house with a broken shoe, they were, so to say, rejoiced. Then, seeing that shoe placed by her in the leather-worker's hand and taking (it) from his hand by a ruse, leaving (it) in a dust-filled road, knowing it (to be his) foot, and seeing the slave-girl entering the courtesan's house in due course, they encircled her dwelling round about.

[99] The stanza is in Prākrit.

[100] I. e., of the completion of the *samasyā*.

[101] Read, with T, *palyāṇyantāṁ* (P, *palāyyantāṁ*; V, *palyayyantāṁ*).

And then immediately the news of recognition (were) made by them to come within the range of Bhoja's hearing. Then the King, with the citizens (and) ministers, went on foot to Vilāsavatī's house. Then Kālidāsa, hearing that, said to Vilāsavatī: 'See, dear, what trouble (is) thine for my sake.' Vilāsavatī: 'Good poet,

> 'Calamity arising for men, (their) whole character is measured therefrom; the wind not blowing, no difference appeareth between a pile of grass and a mountain. (155)
>
> 'On the touchstone of misfortune folk know the worth of friends, kinsmen, relatives, and one's own discernment (and) fortitude. (156)[102]
>
> 'As woe and weal come unbidden to the body, so, methinks, doth misery predominate. (157)

'Good poet, thou driven away a little by the King even with a word, with me this throng of slave-girls will fall into a kindled fire.' Kālidāsa: 'Think not so, dear! Seeing me, Bhoja, with beaming countenance, will fall at (my) feet.' Then Bhoja, entering the courtesan's house, seeing Kālidāsa (and) embracing (him) eagerly, falls at (his) feet. And the King recites:

> [*34*] 'Walking or standing, waking or sleeping, may my thought never be deprived of thee, O poet!' (158)

Kālidāsa, hearing that, stands with face bowed down in shame. And the King, lifting up Kālidāsa's face, said:

> 'Kālidāsa, arts' abode! If, driven slave-like, (I am) wandering here on the King's highway, what shame (is it) for others (to be) there? (159)[103]
>
> 'A fortunate mistress do I deem (Vilāsavatī), since by her, with her own qualities, Kālidāsa (is) enchained like a bird in a cage.' (160)

From (his) eyes the King wipes away a tear of joy with Kālidāsa's hand. Then, gracious through regaining him, the King gave a lakh apiece to the Brāhmans; and mounting Kālidāsa on his own horse, he went with (his) retinue to his own house.

Some time having elapsed, on an occasion the King, looking at the twilight, said:

> 'The sun plungeth into the ocean.'

Then said Bāṇa:

> 'The bee, intoxicated, into the bellies of the lotuses.'

---

[102] = IS 4862; anonymous in Śārṅ. 1438; the preceding stanza also anonymous in Sūk. cx, 42.

[103] I. e., if Bhoja is driven, by his longing to see Kālidāsa, to walk the public road, it is no shame for the poet to be found in a courtesan's house.

Then the poet Maheśvara:

'The bird into the hollow of the tree in the grove.'

Then said Kālidāsa:

'Love slowly, slowly, into maidens.' (161)[104]

The King, pleased, gave a lakh apiece, (but) for the fourth quarter-verse he gave two lakhs.

Upon a time the King saw a Brāhman returning along the road in the outer pleasure-garden. Noticing in his hand a water-jar made of leather and knowing (him to be) very poor, regarding (him) shining with the beauty of (his) countenance (and) stopping (his) horse in front of him, he said: 'Brāhman, why dost thou carry a leathern jar in (thy) hand?' And the Brāhman, reflecting: 'Now (this is) Bhoja because of the beauty of (his) countenance and (his) gentle voice,' said: 'Sire, Bhoja, crest-jewel of the munificent ruling the world, absence of iron (and) copper hath arisen. Therefore do I carry a leathern vessel.' The King: 'Bhoja ruling, what (is) the reason for the non-existence of iron (and) copper?' Then the Brāhman recites:

'Noble Bhoja (being) King, two things (are) very hard to get: iron because of (his) enemies' fetters; copper because of (his) edict-plates.' (162)

[*35*] Then the King, pleased, gave a lakh per syllable.

Upon a time a door-keeper said: 'Lord of Dhārā, a sage come from a far country standeth at the door, and his wife, and his son with his wife.[105] So a sage's family, exceeding purifying, standeth at the door.' The King: 'Oh, full weighty the path of Śāradā's [Sarasvatī's] favour!' At that moment the keeper of the lordly elephants, approaching (and) doing obeisance to the King, said: 'Lord Bhoja, an hundred and twenty-five lordly elephants and sixteen costly gems (have been) sent by the supreme ruler of the land of Siṁhala [Ceylon].' Then said Bāṇa:

'The status of elephants (is) as (that) of poets, whether in their own abode or in a King's abode—are these, like gnats, in every house, their limbs adorned by lords of earth?' (163)

Then the King went out to look at the elephants. Then a Cola[106] scholar, seeing the sage's family, was proud, (thinking:) 'I am the

[104] Anonymous according to Śārṅ. 3588. It should be noted that each quarter-verse rhymes with the others.

[105] He is later named as Vilocana, and each of his family subsequently caps the King's verse (168-171).

[106] The Coromandel Coast (Sanskrit Colamaṇḍala).

King's friend, for I go into the King's palace; but the sage's family remaineth outside, even (though) announced by the door-keeper.' Then the King, knowing (that) pride in his mind, expelled the Cola scholar from the palace-area.

Saying 'Hail!' to the King, one named Taṇḍuladeva, dwelling in the land of Benares, stood (there). And the King asked him: 'Very wise one, where (is thy) dwelling?' Taṇḍuladeva:

> 'In that land I dwell, glorious Lord of Mālava, where existeth the diction (which is) the knife of the tree of stupidity.' (164)[107]

The King, pleased, gave him seven lordly elephants. Then a sage, approaching, said:

> 'Blessings (are) to be gained from penance, but that penance is not found whereby thou, (our) wishing tree,[108] O Bhoja, wilt come within (our) vision's range.' (165)

To him the King gave ten lordly elephants.

Then a Brāhman boy approaches, making the cry 'bhūmbhā.' Then all (were) bewildered; (and) he, brought to the King's presence (and) asked: 'How dost thou make the cry "bhūmbhā?"' said:

> 'Sire, none giveth the support of a hand to poverty sinking in the ocean of thy generosity, O giver of must-elephants!' (166)

[*36*] Then the King, pleased, gave him thirty lordly elephants.

Then enters a sage Vilocana with (his) wife, (and) uttering 'Hail!' he said:

> 'Parvatī, seeing Bhoja giving (his) very own must-elephants, now guardeth again (and) again (her) son [Gaṇeśa], (who hath) the face of a lordly elephant.' (167)

Then the King gave him seven elephants. Then the King, perceiving the sage's family standing before (him) just then, said to the Brāhman:

> 'Success in actions dependeth on (one's own) character, not on assistance from the great.'

The old Brāhman said:

> 'A water-jar (his) birthplace, (his) retinue gazelles, (his) garment birch-bark, (his) abode in a forest, (his) food roots and the like, of such quality (was) Agastya that he put the ocean in the lotus-hollow of (his) hand—

---

[107] Reading *jāḍyaśākhinaḥ* with the Bengali recension (Oster, p. 14); the *rikta-śākhinaḥ* 'of a hollow tree' or 'of an empty Vedist' of the Southern recension is probably corrupt.

[108] Cf. note 3.

success in actions dependeth on (one's own) character, not on assistance from the great.' (168)

Then the King gave him sixteen jewels of great price. Then the King said to his wife: 'Mother, do thou recite!' The lady:

'A single wheel of (his) chariot, seven steeds curbed by serpents, a road with no support, a charioteer without feet, the sun goeth daily to the end of the boundless sky—success in actions dependeth on (one's own) character, not on assistance from the great.' (169)[109]

The King, pleased, gave her seventeen elephants and seven chariots. Then said the King to the Brāhman's son: 'Brāhman's son, do thou recite!' The Brāhman's son:

'Lañkā [Ceylon] to be conquered, the ocean to be crossed on foot, (his) adversary Pulastya's descendant [Rāvaṇa], and monkeys (his) comrades on the battle-field, he [Rāma], on foot (and) a mortal, slew all the Rākṣaka-race—success in actions dependeth on (one's own) character, not on assistance from the great.' (170)

The King, pleased, gave the Brāhman's son eighteen lordly elephants. Then, seeing the Brāhman's daughter-in-law adorned with every part of (her) limbs very delicate (and) charming, as if with a form produced by the erotic sentiment,[110] (and) with a lovely slender body like a champak-tendril, (and) in mind doing (her) the homage: 'Now this (is) some sportive form of Bhāratī [Sarasvatī],' the King said: 'Mother, pronounce a benediction!' [*37*] The Brāhman's daughter-in-law: 'Harken, Sire:

'(His) bow of flowers, (his) bow-cord of bees, (his) arrow the corner of the eyes of fleeting-eyed (women), (his) friend the chill-souled maker of cold [the moon], and himself alone, Love confoundeth all the world—success in actions dependeth on (one's own) character, not on assistance from the great.' (171)

The King, amazed, taking all Queen Līlā's adornments, gave (them) to her, and (also) bestowed gold, pearls, cat's-eyes, and coral.

Then upon a time a poet named Sīmanta said:

'"Road, shorten (thy) length! Sun, abandon (thy) hard glare! glorious Mount Vindhya, mercifully be gracious, straightway be nigh!" Thus, glorious Bhoja, thine enemies daily stammer and swoon, seeing their beloved weary with far flight.' (172)

At that very instant a goldsmith, taking a golden dish adorned with rubies on the edges, left (it) before the King. Then said the King

[109] = IS 5712; ascribed to Arghaṭa in Subhāṣ. 2277; stanza 170 to an anonymous Brāhman in Vikrama. JR III a, 3.

[110] Cf. Regnaud, pp. 301-306.

to the poet Sīmanta: 'Good poet, this dish showeth a certain beauty.' Then said the poet:

> 'Lord of Dhārā, the Master of Lights [the sun], conquered by thy splendour, serveth thee, Sire, under the guise of a golden dish.' (173)

Then the King, pleased, gave (him) that very dish, filling it with pearls.

Upon a time the King, through pleasure in the chase, seeing a boar fleeing before (him), penetrated alone by himself into a forest. There perceiving a most excellent Brāhman, he said: 'Brāhman, whither wilt thou go?' The Brāhman: 'To the city of Dhārā.' Bhoja: 'Why?' The Brāhman: 'To see Bhoja through desire of wealth. He giveth to a scholar; I myself ask not of a fool.' Bhoja: 'Brāhman, (art) thou then a sage or a poet?' The Brāhman: 'Right fortunate one, I (am) a poet.' Bhoja: 'Then recite somewhat.' The Brāhman: 'None but Bhoja knoweth the way of my verse.' [*38*] The King: 'Even I have knowledge of immortal diction, and the King liketh me, and I shall make thy talent known; show some skill in art.' The Brāhman: 'What do I describe?' The King: 'Describe this rice.' The Brāhman:

> 'Rice, bent down with ripeness, the surface of (its) roots perfumed with fragrant water-lilies, (its) head trembling in the breeze, mostly maketh praise of redolence.' (174)

Taking off all (his) adornments, the King gave (them) to him.

Then upon a time a potter's wife, coming to the King's palace, said to the door-keeper: 'Door-keeper, the King must be seen.' He said: 'What (is) thy business with the King?' She said: 'I shall not tell thee; only before the King do I explain (it).' He, going to the court, said: 'Sire, a potter's wife, desirous of seeing the King, doth not tell (her) business before me; before thee will she explain (it).' The King: 'Let her enter'; and she, approaching (and) making obeisance, says:

> 'Sire, from digging in the earth a treasure (hath been) seen by my beloved; he, simply seeing (it), remaineth there; I have come to tell thee.' (175)

And the King, astonished, had the treasure-jar brought. When the King, opening its stopper, looks, seeing the radiant mass of wealth (and) jewels therein, he asks the potter: 'What (is) this, potter?' And he said:

> 'Beholding (their) King Moon, even thee, come to earth's surface, the stars, methinks, have descended under the guise of a multitude of gems.' (176)

The King, hearing (that) amazing stanza from the potter's mouth, astounded, gave him all.

Then upon a time the King roved about everywhere alone at night, seeing the behaviour of the city and listening to the conversation of the citizens. Then somewhere in a Vaiśya's house a Vaiśya said to his darling: 'Darling, the King, though enamoured of very scant giving, desireth pre-eminence over Vikramārka, lord of the city of Ujjain.[111] Is this gained by Bhoja? Bhoja (hath been) brought to greatness by certain poets, Mayūra and the rest, devoted to laudation; but Bhoja is (only) Bhoja. Harken, dear:

> 'If a dog (have) a factitious mane fastened to (his) hairy shoulder-blade and (be) promoted to the status of a foe of beasts [the lion], [*39*] eager to cleave the sloping lobes of must-elephants, how will he make the roar of a deer-king?' (177)[112]

The King, hearing (this), reflected: 'This (man) sayeth very sooth.' Then he hears (him) saying again (and) again:

> 'The unfortunate (is) indeed a vessel (for generosity, but the mere) utterance, "Give (to me" is) not (a proof of) learning; just (what is) appropriate should be given; how (is) thy generosity, Vikramārka, to be described? (178)[113]
>
> 'By thee, glorious Vikramārka, an hundred and eight villages (were) given to a Brāhman's son asking (of thee); where in Bhoja (is) thy greatness? (179)
>
> 'Even a potter attaineth to the greatness of Prajāpati[114] if, Vikrama, Bhoja attaineth to pre-eminence over thee.' (180)

The King: 'Every man on earth fearlessly speaketh truth in his own house. Neither by me nor by another can pre-eminence over Vikramārka in any way be gained.'

Then upon a time a poet, coming to the King's door, said: 'The King must be seen.' Then, admitted, saying 'Hail!' to the King, (and) seated at his command, he recites:

> 'Among poets, speakers, voluptuaries,[115] (ordinary) men, mighty, benefactors

---

[111] Vikramārka, Vikramāditya, or simply Vikrama is probably to be identified with Candragupta II (*c.* 375-413), famous both as a warrior and as a patron of letters. Among the 'nine gems' ascribed to his court were Kālidāsa and Vararuci, who also are made by Ballāla to appear at the court of Bhoja (!).

[112] Ascribed to Bhallaṭa in Subhāṣ. 995.

[113] The learned (Brāhmans, poets, etc.) have the right to ask for alms and rewards; the request of an ordinary man, merely because he is unfortunate, must be judged on its own merits.

[114] The 'Lord of Creatures,' the Creator.

[115] In the Indian scheme of life, love (*kāma*) ranks equally with practical affairs (*artha*) and duty (*dharma*).

of the good, rich, archers, (and) them (whose) treasure (is) duty, (there is) on earth's surface no King equal to Bhoja.' (181)

The King bestowed a lakh on him, (and) taking off all (his) adornments, he gave (them to him), and (also) a horse.[116]

Then upon a time the King, going to the pleasure-grove (and) seeing with (his) eyes a beautiful-eyed (woman) in the mid-road with a garment of soiled thread (and) with the lotus of (her) countenance burned by the beams of the hot-rayed (sun), he asked:

'Who (art) thou, daughter?'

And she, knowing by the beauty of (his) countenance (that he was) glorious Bhoja, ruler of the earth, delighted, said:

'A hunter's wife, Lord of Men.'

Filled with joy, the King said to her, with a series of skilful connexions:

'What (is) this in (thy) hand?'

[*40*] And she said:

'Meat.'

The King said:

'Why (is it) lean?'

And she said:

'If 'tis heard respectfully, I tell (it) candidly, Lord of Men.

'On the banks of streams of tears of thy foes' wives the Siddha-women sing;[117] blind with (their) song, the deer graze not; therefore (is) meat lean.' (182)

The King gave her a lakh per syllable

Then, going home, he [Bhoja] (was) seated in an *œil-de-bœuf*. And seeing Bhoja sitting there, a man, standing in the King's highway, said: 'Harken, Sire, Protector of All the World:

'The dike (hath its) bank broken within by the waters both on this side and on that; the earth (is) hard to traverse; this mountain (hath) much miry snow; the rite of lustration of elephants (and) horses[118] now completed, I know not (where) thine enemies will go nor by what road.' (183)

[116] T omits mention of the horse.

[117] The Siddhas, 88,000 in number, are semi-divine beings dwelling between earth and heaven, north of the sun and south of the Great Bear. Instead of P's *durbalam* 'weak, lean,' V and T read *durlabham* 'hard to get, scarce.'

[118] For a projected military expedition by Bhoja.

Bhoja, pleased, gave him, just standing on the road, five pedigreed elephants.

Upon a time the King, devoted to the pleasures of the chase, mounting (his) steed, set forth.

> Then, knowing by (his) dress (that a man who had) crossed a river with fuel lifted on (his) head (was) a Brāhman, the King quickly asked: (184)
>
> 'How deep (is) the water, Brāhman?'

He said:

> 'Reaching to the knee, Lord of Men.'

The King astonished, said:

> 'Why (is) thy condition thus?'

He said:

> 'All (are) not like Thy Majesty.' (185)[119]

Out of curiosity the King said: 'Sage, ask a lakh of the comptroller of the treasury; it will be given (thee) by my word.' Then the sage, throwing the wood on the ground (and) going to the comptroller of the treasury, said: 'I (am) sent by the Great King; let a lakh be given me.' Then he said, laughing: 'Thine Honour's appearance is not worth a lakh.' Then he, going dejected to the King, said: [*41*] 'He laugheth again, Sire; he giveth not.' Then out of curiosity the King said: 'Ask two lakhs; they will be given.' Again going, the Brāhman said: 'The King saith that two lakhs are to be given.' Again he laughs. Again reaching Bhoja, the Brāhman said: 'That most evil (fellow) laugheth at me; he giveth not.' Then glorious Bhojarāja, ruling the earth, curious, (and) the abode of sportiveness, said 'Brāhman, ask three lakhs; necessarily he will give (them).' He, going again, said: 'The King hath three lakhs given me.' Again he laughs. Then the Brāhman, angered, again going (to Bhoja), said: 'Sire, he giveth not.

> 'O King, while thou art raining everywhere with streams of gold, not (even) drops come on me, covered with an umbrella of misfortune. (186)[120]
>
> 'While thou, the cloud, art raining, all trees (are) in bud; (there is) doubt as to the old leaves of us *arka*-trees. (187)[121]
>
> 'One effort (and) then one effort of this one [me] (the comptroller of the

---

[119] Cf. IS 7501 = Mer. 66 (Taw. 37-38), from whom the whole episode is borrowed.

[120] = IS 5738 = stanza 314, there spoken by Kaviśekhara.

[121] The rain brings out the new foliage, but may make the old leaves of the *arka* (Calotropis Gigantea) fall. The cloud here, as in many other stanzas, refers to Bhoja, who rains gifts as the cloud pours down water.

treasury casteth out); shamelessness of an inferior object [myself] (rusheth forth): blind darkness by the sun is cast out; constantly it rusheth forth.' (188)[122]

Then said the King:

'Be not wroth because of my word; going to the comptroller of the treasury, three lakhs and ten lordly elephants (are) to be taken by thee, O Twice-Born.' (189)

Then he sends a body-guard. Then the comptroller of the treasury writes in the religious (account) book:

'A lakh, a lakh, (and) again, a lakh, and ten must-elephants (have been) given by Bhoja, pleased by the saying, "Reaching to the knee."' (190)[123]

Then, glorious Bhoja, lord of men, adorning the lion-throne, a door-keeper, approaching, said: 'O King, a poet named Śukadeva, derided because of poverty, is at the door.' The King said to Bāṇa: 'Most excellent scholar, good poet, dost thou know (his) character?' Bāṇa: 'Sire, only Kālidāsa knoweth the adequacy of Śukadeva's knowledge, no one else.' The King said: 'Good poet, friend Kālidāsa, dost thou know the poet Śukadeva?' Kālidāsa: 'Sire,

'In all the earth I know two good poets: Bhavabhūti and this Śuka; Vālmīki[124] (is) the third of them two.' (191)

[*42*] Then said Sītā, lauded by the poet-throng:

'What a kronking don't crows make hither and yon! But the parrot[125] speaketh (only when) caressed by the Royal hand.' (192)

Then said Mayūra:

'A man who, unasked, sayeth aught in the King's court receiveth not merely disrespect, (but) also derision. (193)[126]

'Thus is it said, Sire:

'(Without Śukadeva) what (is) a court? What (is) poets' knowledge? Who (are) poets of taste? What, in sooth, (is) thy generosity, Bhoja, whereby this Śuka is pleased? (194)

'So let Śukadeva, come to the palace-door, be brought into the court.'

[122] The second distich means that the darkness of the poet's poverty is constantly dissipated by the radiance of Bhoja's generosity, but that it as constantly returns through the treasurer's refusal to give what the King has promised.

[123] Mer. 66 (Taw. 38); see stanza 185.

[124] The author of the *Rāmāyaṇa.*

[125] *Śuka,* a play on the poet's name, Śukadeva.

[126] Cf. IS 453.

Then the King reflects. Hearing of the adequacy of Śukadeva, he was filled with joy and dejection: joy that a great poet (had been) seen, and dejection (as to) what should be given to that topmost crest-jewel of good poets. 'Very well! Door-keeper, let (him) enter!' Then the King, seeing Śukadeva approaching, descended from (his) lion-throne. All the scholars, making obeisance to Śukadeva, courteously made (him) enter; and the King, seating him on the lion-throne, himself sat down at his bidding. Then said Śukadeva: 'Sire, Lord of Dhārā, the glory in giving which (is) the noble Vikrama's, lord of men, in sooth honoureth thee. Sire, rich indeed (is) the Lord of Mālava [Bhoja], (but) no other princes, with whom these great poets, Kālidāsa and the rest, abide like birds cord-bound.' Then he recites:

> 'Through fear of Bhoja's splendour the sun hath become (his) friend; the submarine fire[127] assumeth a mare's form; the lightning (hath) become (but) momentary.' (195)

The King: 'Stay, good poet, let no further distich be recited.'

> 'Unto Śuka Bhoja, pleased, gave a golden jar with wondrous rubies filled, and elephants four hundred.' (196)

So writing in the religious (account) book, and giving (it) all, the comptroller of the treasury dismissed Śuka. The King, knowing (that) Śuka (was) gone to his own land, rejoiced, and the assembly (were) pleased.

On another occasion, in the rainy season, a poet named Vāsudeva, approaching, saw the King. The King: 'Good poet, describe the rain-cloud.' Then said the poet:

> [*43*] 'Not by thought-gems, not by wish-trees, not by the Cow of Plenty[128] and the rest, and not by gods, great or even small, devoted to the welfare of others, O cloud, doth the world, methinks, live here, (but) by thee, ceaselessly sprinkling the earth with masses of water (and), fit to bear the burden, even to-day carrying the load.' (197)

The King gave a lakh.

Upon a time the prime minister,[129] seeing the King constantly giving,

[127] *Aurva*, the fiery wrath of the ṛṣi Aurva, cast by him, to save the world from destruction, into Vaḍabāmukha ('Mare's Mouth'), a cavern under the ocean at the South Pole.

[128] 'Thought-gems' (*cintāmaṇi*), 'wish-trees' (*kalpataru*), and the 'Cow of Plenty' (*Kāmadhenu*), produced at the Churning of the Ocean, were supposed to grant every desire.

[129] Named Rohaka in Mer. 64 (Taw. 36-37); cf. IS 959.

(but) unable to speak, wrote clear letters on the wall of the King's bed-chamber:

'Because of (possible) misfortune one should guard wealth.'

The King, rising from bed, (and) going (and) seeing these letters, himself wrote the second quarter-verse:

'Whence (are) the misfortunes of the glorious?'

The next day, the minister, seeing the second quarter-verse written, himself wrote the third:

'If that fortune (be) departed,'

On the morrow the King writes the fourth quarter-verse:

'Wealth accumulated perisheth.' (198)

Then the prime minister falls at the King's feet, (saying:) 'Sire, this my transgression must be forgiven.'

On another occasion a certain Brāhman's thief,[130] thinking (that) the Lord of Dhārā (was) sleeping in an upper storey of the palace, entering the King's treasury—an ingress being first dug—taking many jewels of divers sorts, cat's-eyes and the like, (but) thinking (that) these (were) each a debt to the Other World, (and) right there attaining indifference (to mundane objects), reflected:

'The lame and leprous, the blind and crippled, (and) the poor embodied eat the fruit of evil previously acquired.' (199)

Then on (his) lordly couch at the end of sleep, beholding the lovely throng of (his) wives adorned with divers jewels (and) bracelets, and reflecting on all (his) elephants, horses, chariots, (and) foot-soldiers, delighted with (his) Royal fortune, the King said, from the greatness of (his) joy:

'Mind-ravishing (are) young women; friends (are) harmonious; (there are) good kinsfolk; and servants (have) words full of devotion; the herds of elephants dance; spirited (are) the horses.'

Thus three lines (were) spoken by the King; the fourth line does not come forth from the King's mouth. Then (it was) completed by the thief, hearing this:

[*44*] 'At the closing of the eyes (in death) there is naught whatsoever.' (200)[131]

---

[130] According to Mer. 75 (Taw. 43), this Brāhman was Rājaśekhara, but in Sad. IV, xxiii, 5, his poem (stanza 201) is ascribed to Cittapa, in Śārṅ. 777 to Akālajalada, and in Subhāṣ. 843 to Dākṣiṇātya.

[131] Ascribed to Vikramāditya in Subhāṣ. 3318.

Then the King, (having) the stanza composed (and) seeing the thief, gave him a hero's bracelet. Then the thief, going with the bracelet to the Brāhman's house, rousing the Brāhman, (who was) lying down, (and) giving (it) to him, said: 'Brāhman, this hand-bracelet of the King (is) of great price (and) should not be sold for a small price.' Then the Brāhman, selling it in the market-place, got magnificent ornaments and turban-cloths. Then some of the Royal retainers, thinking him [the Brāhman] (to be) the thief, inform the King. Then he (was) brought to the King's presence. The King asks: 'Brāhman, not even a cloth should be worn (by thee); whence (are these) magnificent earrings, ornaments, (and) turban-cloths early indeed to-day?' The Brāhman said:

> 'In that dry pool (were they found) in which (water was) dead, as it were, because of frogs resting in the hollows of trees, with tortoises gone underground (and) constantly coagulated by sheat-fish from (their) wallowing in (their) bed of thick mire; (but) that (is now) set in motion by a cloud come out of season, (and) where water is drunk by herds of wild elephants submerged up to (their) frontal lobes.' (201)

The King, delighted (at) ascertaining (that) the hero's bracelet (had been) given by the thief to him [the Brāhman], himself gave him a lakh.

In another occasion a lord of poets named Viṣṇu, coming to the King's door, admitted (and) seeing the King, said, with a preliminary 'Hail':

> 'Lord of Dhārā! The line that the Creator, eager to reckon the mighty lords of earth, drew in the sky with a bit of chalk in his reckoning of thee, that, in sooth, became this river of the Thrice-Ten (Gods [the Ganges]); but, because of the absence of world-lords equal to thee, he threw the chalk away—that (is) this Snow-Mountain [the Himālaya] on earth's pedestal.' (202)[132]

The King, hearing the marvellous poem, reflected: 'What should be given?' At that instant, harkening to such unrivalled poetry, the face of a poet named Somanātha became pale. Then, out of wickedness, he said to the King: 'Sire, this is a good poet, but never is the King's court seen by him, since he (is) an ocean of poverty and hath not even an out-worn loin-cloth.' Then the King said to Somanātha:

> 'If (there are) irreproachable verses of a lordless man, what harm (is it)? Would a sugar-cane be flavourless (even though) stuck by a beggar in (his) armpit?' (203)[133]

Then, giving betel to all, the King rose from the court. Then all

[132] Ascribed to Dhanapāla in Mer. 101 (Taw. 61).

[133] = IS 3745; to Bhavabhūti in Śārṅ. 148 and Sūk. iv, 29; cf. the anomalous and suspicious position of the 'landless man' in the feudal system.

said, one to the other: 'Hearing the poesy of the poet Viṣṇu, [*45*] perfect wickedness hath been committed by Somanātha to-day.' Then the assembly of sages arose. Then the poet Viṣṇu, writing a stanza on a leaf, giving (it) in Somanātha's hand, (and) bowing, started to go (saying:) 'Do thou, indeed, long rejoice here in the court.' Then the poet Somanātha reads:

> 'If, O cloud, thou releasest not water on these trees devoured by forest-fires fanned by fresh winds, release (it) not; but why, pitiless one, hurlest thou a thunderbolt?' (204)[134]

Then the poet Somanātha gave (Viṣṇu) all (his) fortune, consisting of turban-cloths, wealth, gold, horses, and the like, excepting a dress for (his) wife.

Then the King, bent on the pleasure of the chase, going along (and) seeing the poet Viṣṇu, reflected: 'I (have) not even given him food. Not respecting me, he will go to his own land filled with wealth. I ask him: "Poet Viṣṇu, whence (hath this) wealth (been) acquired?"' The poet said:

> 'Through Somanātha, a beggar at thy house, Sire, Mighty One of Kings, (there hath been) the full illusion of the wishing-tree to-day in (the case of) me, most piteous.' (205)

The King gave a lakh per syllable for the poem previously heard in the court, and he gave as much to Somanātha as (had been) given by Somanātha. Somanātha said:

> 'Whence (are) the buds or the flowers, and, likewise, where the fruits of the forest-shrubs when this cloud, causelessly compassionate, bestoweth not the waters here?' (206)

Then the poet Viṣṇu (was) delighted with (what was) given by Somanātha and given by the King. Then said the poet Sīmanta:

> 'Śeṣa [the cosmic serpent] beareth the series of worlds on the flat surface of (his) hood; and he is always borne by the Lord of Tortoises on the middle of (his) back; him, in sooth, the ocean carefully maketh resting on (his) bosom. Oh, boundless (are) the powers of the activity of the great!' (207)[135]

Upon a time a retainer, approaching the King on the palace-roof, said: 'Sire, all the mass of wealth without exception there is in the treasuries (hath been) given by (My) Lord to poets. Moreover, [*46*] there is not even a bit of wealth in the treasure-house. Every day some poet standeth

[134] Ascribed to Viśveśvara in Sad. IV, lxii, 5.

[135] = IS 6012 (Bhartṛhari i, 35).

at the door. (It hath been) said that the prime minister should proclaim in (My) Lord's presence that henceforth no poet or sage whosoever should (be) admitted to the King.' Even (though) knowing (that) all in the treasury (had been) given, the King said: 'To-day let a poet standing at the door enter.' Then a sage,[136] approaching (and) saying 'Hail!' spoke:

> 'O cloud, be (thy) streams of water afar indeed! Even thy sweet thunder (is) not heard by the *cātaka* long sitting in a supportless sky with the concave hollow of (his) beak upturned to thee.' (208)[137]

Hearing that, (saying:) 'Fie on life, since sages and poets, coming to (my) door, sit there,' (and) stripping off all (his) adornments, the King gave (them) to the Brāhman.

Then the King, summoning the comptroller of the treasury, said: 'Treasurer, where (are) the jars filled with jewels amid those treasures which (were) King Muñja's (and) so (are) mine and former (monarchs')?' Then a poet Mucukunda from the land of Kāśmīr, coming and saying 'Hail!' spoke:

> 'O Bhoja, as if from fear of submission in the ocean of thy glory the cloud depositeth two jars under the pretext of disks of the sun (and) moon.' (209)[138]

The King gave him a lakh per syllable. Again the poet said:

> 'As many tears of the *cātaka* (as) were lost for thee, O cloud, so many drops of water (were) not released by thee, generous[139] one!' (210)

Then the King gave him an hundred horses. Then the treasurer writes:

> 'To the poet Mucukunda he gave an hundred thoroughbred horses; even having given a lakh, Bhoja is again importuned by him.' (211)

Then the King, having sent all home, goes in. Then the King's chowry-bearer said:

> 'O King, light of Muñja's race, crest-jewel of all the monarchs of earth! Thy course (is) conjoined in the night with a parasol of marvellous jewels [the stars]; let not the moon be bowed with shame at the sight of thy face,

---

[136] V adds 'named Śrīpati.'

[137] = IS 3360 (*Cātakāṣṭaka* i, 8, ed. Haeberlin, p. 238); ascribed to Acalasiṁha in Sad. IV, lxiii, 2; anonymous in Sūk. xiii, 2. The *cātaka* (Cuculus Melanoleucus) is conventionally supposed to subsist only on rain-drops.

[138] Ascribed to Jayavardhana in Subhāṣ. 2478, with change of *rājan* to *Bhoja*, as frequently in Ballāla's work (Oster, p. 36).

[139] Sarcastic!

and let not this glorious Arundhatī become a vessel of ill behaviour!' (212)[140]

To her the King gave a lakh per syllable.

[47] On another occasion a poet named Gopāla, coming from the city of Kuṇḍina,[141] said, with a preliminary 'Hail!':

'Two things come forth in thy mind, Bhoja, are (as) blades of grass: in (thy) wrath an army of foes, in (thy) graciousness a pile of gold.' (213)

Though hearing (this and) pleased, the King will not give. With the Royal retainers he [Gopāla] stands pondering. Then the poet reflected: 'Hasn't the King heard?' Then, suddenly seeing (him) exalted, the poet said to the King:

'O cloud, as the quarter (of the sky) is everywhere hid by Thy Majesty on high, so, methinks, steadfast one, thou wilt indeed make a pool like to the Ocean of Milk; but not even for an instant doth this shoal of sheat-fish and the like endure, distressed by summer's heat (and) with thee (their) only refuge; so rain at least a little bit!' (214)

Knowing the poet's heart (and) saying: 'Poet Gopāla, thou art exceeding burnt by the fire of poverty,' the King gave (him) sixteen priceless gems and sixteen lordly elephants.

Upon a time the King, roving about in the city of Dhārā, saw two men sleeping somewhere in a temple of Śiva. One of them, (his) sleep departed, says: 'O thou right near my rug, who (art) thou? Hast thou (been) asleep? Art thou awake or not?' Then the other said: 'Brāhman, I am bowed before (thee). I (am) a Brāhman's son. Seeing thee lying here at nightfall and, the light lit, knowing (thee to be) a Brāhman by (thy) water-jar, sacred cord, and so on, I slept near Thine Honour's rug. Now, hearing thy voice, I (am) awake.' The first said: 'Dear (sir), if thou (art) bowed before (me), then be thou long-lived. Tell whence thou hast come, what thy name, and what (thy) business here.' The second said: 'Brāhman, my name (is) Bhāskara; my abode, nigh the Prabhāsatīrtha on the shore of the Western Ocean. There the generosity of Bhoja (hath been) described by many; hence I (have) come to beg. Because of (thine) age, thou art like a father to me. Do thou make (me) well acquainted (with thyself).' He said: 'Dear (sir), my name is Śākalya. I have come from the city of Ekaśilā to Bhoja through hope of wealth. Dear (sir), misfortune is recognised in

[140] Arundhatī, the wife of Vasiṣṭha (later of Dharma), was noted for her chastity; also, as here, the wife of the Seven Ṛṣis (the seven stars of Ursa Major).

[141] The capital of Berar, identified with the modern Kundapur or with Kondavir.

thee even untold by thee. Tell (me) of what nature (is) such wretchedness.' Then said Bhāskara: 'Father, how tell I (my) misfortune?

> '(My) children hunger-thin like corpses, (my) kindred with exceeding indifferent intentions (on my behalf, and) the rattle of a drum smeared with bits of lac distress me not so much [*48*] as the angry wife of folk in every house (when) asked by me, smiling with a plaintive note, for a needle to mend the torn garment of my spouse.' (215)

Hearing (this), taking off all (his) adornments, (and) giving (them) to him, the King said: 'Bhāskara, thy children are exceeding distressed. Go straightway to (thine own) land.' Then said Śākalya:

> 'Exceeding high the earth (is) lifted; cloven (is) the host of foes; by the Mighty One [Bhoja] the glory of mighty kings (is) made a jest; what the Primeval Man did in three births (hath been) done by this youth in a single birth.' (216)[142]

Then the King gave Śākalya three lakhs.

On another occasion the King (was) roving about with enjoyment of the chase. There a poet,[143] with hope of wealth, said to him, a gazelle (that had) come before (him) pierced with an arrow:

> 'Noble Bhoja gone to hunt, the bow straightway strung (and) drawn to the tip of (his) ear, the arrow passed from (his) clenched hand and clinging to (his quarry's) body, (there is) no flight from (her) place, no motion, no trembling, no leaping up because of the gazelle's hope: "This (God of) Love putteth (my) darling in my power."' (217)[144]

The King gave him three lakhs.

On another occasion, noble King Bhoja adorning the lion-throne, a door-keeper coming, said: 'Sire, an aged learned Brāhmaness, dwelling on the bank of the Jāhnavī [Ganges], standeth at the door.' The King: 'Let (her) enter.' Then the King bows before (her), approaching; and she, saying to him: 'Live long!' spoke:

> 'This unprecedented fire of Bhoja's splendour awaketh in the places of kings' encampments, which entered in, grasses grow in the courts of the houses of enemy princes.' (218)[145]

---

[142] Ascribed to Dhanapāla in Mer. 95 (Taw. 57). The Primeval Man is Viṣṇu, who, in his Boar-Incarnation, upraised the earth, as Paraśurāma slew his foes, and in his Dwarf-Incarnation strode over the earth in three steps. The preceding stanza is anonymous in Sad. V, xlviii, 3.

[143] V adds his name, Gālava.

[144] Bhoja, transfixing the gazelle with an arrow, is taken by her to be Kāma, whose arrow, piercing the heart of the beloved, inspires with love.

[145] Oster (p. 36) notes that this stanza is taken from its context in Bilhaṇa's *Vikramāñkadevacarita*, with the substitution of Bhoja's name for Vikrama's.

The King gives her a jar full of jewels. Then the treasurer writes:

> 'By Bhoja, pleased with the laudation of (his) splendour, a jar full of gold (and) gems (was) given to the aged woman in the King's court.' (219)

On another occasion a thief come from a far country said to the King: 'Sire, in the land of Siṁhala [Ceylon] a Royal maiden (was) seen by me in a temple of Cāmuṇḍā [Durgā]. And she, seeing me, [*49*] asked: "The greatness of the lord of the land of Mālava (hath been) heard many times; do thou tell (it)." And by me (My) Lord's virtues (were) described to her. And she, from excessive joy, giving (me) an incomparable bit from the interior of a sandal-tree, went to her own place. So take this, Sire, (which hath been) obtained by the description of (thy) virtues. Because of the abundance of perfume proceeding from this, bees and serpents come together.' The King, taking it (and) delighted, gave him a lakh. Then, under the guise of it, the poet Dāmodara praises the King:

> 'Glorious sandal-tree! Many are those trees in the forest whose whole perfume resideth chiefly in the beauty of (their) flowers; this virtue of fragrance, proclaimed (and) declared in every part by thee, that fine, pure, famous soul—where (else) is it seen here?' (220)

The King, recognising laudation of himself, gave a lakh.

Then a door-keeper, approaching, said: 'Sire, a stage-manager's wife is at the door.' The King: 'Let (her) enter.' Then, approaching (and) making obeisance to the King, she said:

> 'Bali,[146] dwelling in Pātāla (and) put below—what marvel (is there) in that? The wishing-tree, even (though) standing in heaven, (but) put below by thee—(that is) a marvel.' (221)

The King gave her a lakh per syllable.

Then upon a time the King, utterly wearied in hunting, stood somewhere below a fragrant mango-tree. There a poet named Mallinātha, approaching, said:

> 'How many trees are there not in the forest wide-extended with hundreds (and) hundreds of branches? Few (are) the trees (whose) leaves (are) cloven by swarms of bees assembling because of the abundance of (their) perfume.' (222)[147]

---

[146] A Daitya (one of a class of demons) whose devotion and penance were such that he gained authority over the three worlds of heaven, earth, and the infernal regions (Pātāla). The gods accordingly appealed to Viṣṇu, who, in his Dwarf-Incarnation (see note 142), obtained from Bali as much land as he could cover in three steps. In two, he strode over earth and heaven, but, in consideration of Bali's virtues, left him sovereignty over Pātāla. For the wishing-tree see note 3.

[147] Ascribed to Vaidyabhānu in Sūk. xxxiii, 1, and Śārṅ. 973.

Then the King gave him a wrist-bracelet.

The King sitting right there, a sage, approaching (and) uttering 'Hail!' said: 'O King, beginning with the land of Benares, I, a dweller in an exhausted land, wander on pilgrimage to *tīrthas*.'[148] The King: 'From the sight of (folk) like Thine Honour, dwelling at *tīrthas*, I am content.' He said: 'And we[149] (are) sorcerers.' The King: 'Among Brāhmans everything is possible.' Again the King said: 'Brāhman, as through knowledge of spells (there is) attainment of the fruit (of acts in this life) in the Other World, what is there in this world?' The Brāhman: 'O King, acquisition of knowledge from adoration of Sarasvatī's feet (is) known to all; but acquisition of wealth (is) dependent on luck.

> 'Virtues, indeed, (are) just virtues; virtues (are) not causes of prosperity; luck making accumulation of wealth (is a thing) apart. (223)[150]

[*50*] 'Sire, virtues of knowledge exist for the foundation of the worlds, not merely of prosperity. Sire,

> 'The aggregate of virtues dependent on one's self, lack of virtue (is) reprehensibility; wealth dependent on Fate, what blame (is there) of men (if it existeth not)? (224)

'Sire, through propitiation by spells power would be irresistible. Sire, behold a curious thing:[151] through Sarasvatī's favour, he on whose head a hand is laid by me would have an uninterrupted extension of knowledge.' The King said: 'O very wise one, great (is) the power of the goddess!' Then the King, summoning a slave-girl, said to the Brāhman: 'Best of Twice-Born, lay (thy) hand on this courtesan's head.' The Brāhman, laying (his) hand on her head, said to her: 'Lady, tell what the King bids.' Then said the slave-girl: 'Sire, to-day I behold, like a myrobalan in my hand,[152] all (that is) born of eloquence. Sire, command (me). What do I describe?' Then the King, again regarding (his) sword, said: 'Describe my sword.' The slave-girl said:

> 'The falchion, this thy sword, Lord of Men, (is) a marvellous thing; the eyes of (thine) enemies' wives rain (tears); continually (there is) disunion with (its) sheath in battle; the poverty of hostile princes increaseth.' (225)[153]

---

[148] Pilgrim bathing-places on the banks of sacred streams.

[149] 'Editorial we' = 'I.'

[150] = IS 2129 = Subhāṣ. 2672.

[151] Reading *ekaṁ kutūhalaṁ paśya* with T; P *evaṁ kutūhalaṁ yasya*; so V, but omitting the senseless *yasya*.

[152] See note 31.

[153] *Dhārādhara* may mean 'cloud' (cf. the 'rain' of the second verse) as well

The King gave her five priceless jars of jewels.

Then at that instant five poets gathered from somewhere. Looking at them (and) seeing the King's face a little in the shade, the poet Maheśvara said, under the guise of a tree:

> 'Why art thou born at a cross-road? Thou hast very thick shade; why (art thou) with shade? If (thou art) hidden, why art thou fruitful? Thou art full of the burdens of fruit; why (art thou) bowed down? O good tree, through thine own errors long endure now the dragging, shaking, cracking, (and) breaking of the tips of (thy) branches by folk!' (226)[154]

Then the King gave him a lakh. Then those best of the Twice-Born, each separately uttering a benediction (and) one after the other donning a woolen garment at the King's bidding, gave a blessing. Then one (of them [Kāmadeva]) recites:

> 'Let the Tortoise sport in the water of the Ganges in Pātāla; let the Primal Boar take the nutgrass growing on (its) banks; let the Lord of Serpents [Śeṣa] relax the circle of (his) hood; [*51*] let the Elephants of the (Eight) Quarters swallow the lotus-roots; let all the lordly mountains wander at will whilst thou, Prince Bhoja, sustainest the Goddess Earth.' (227)[155]

The King, astonished, gave him an hundred horses. Then the treasurer writes:

> 'In the pleasure-garden an hundred horses, swift as thought, (were) given by the Lord of Men to Kāmadeva under the fragrant mango-tree.' (228)

Then upon a time Bhoja reflected: 'No one is (as) bountiful as I.' The prime minister, knowing his pride, showed Bhoja Vikramārka's religious (account) book. In that book Bhoja saw an allusion as follows: because of thirst, Vikramārka said:

> 'Let water be brought, clear as the thought of good folk, very light as the pain of the wretched,[156] cool as the embrace of sons, also sweet as (their) prattling in their infancy, shining with cardamons, cuscus, cloves, (and) sandal, (and) perfumed with camphor, musk, nutmegs, trumpet-flowers, (and) screw-pines.' (229)

---

as 'falchion,' and contains an obvious allusion to Bhoja as 'Lord of Dhārā'; *kośa* means both 'sheath' ('disunion with its sheath'), referring to Bhoja's drawn sword, and 'treasure' ('disunion with [their] treasure'), alluding to the poverty of Bhoja's foes cut off from their treasuries.

[154] = IS 7500; ascribed to Bhadantajñānavarman in Sūk. xxxiii, 4, and Śārṅ. 971; anonymous in Sad. IV, lvi, 5. As applicable to Bhoja, the cross-road refers to his accessibility to all; the shade and the fruit, to his liberality to the poor; his errors, to the fact that he is so generous.

[155] The Tortoise and the Boar are two of the incarnations of Viṣṇu.

[156] I. e., in Vikramāditya's reign the wretched suffer very little.

Then said the court-panegyrist:

> 'Sarasvatī [the goddess of speech, or, the river Sarasvatī] always inhabiteth (thy) lotus-mouth; red [or, the river Son] (is) thy lip; thy right arm, skilful in making remembrances of the heroism of Kakutstha's scion [Rāma] hath a signet [or, is the ocean]; how do the armies [or, these rivers] come, not constantly leave thy side? Tell whence, O King, in thy clear mind arose the desire for drinking water!' (230)[157]

Then spoke Vikramārka thus:

> 'Eight ten-millions of gold (pieces), ninety-three balances[158] of pearls, fifty elephants with bees intoxicated by the sweet perfume (of their ichor and) roused to fury, a myriad of horses, (and) an hundred courtesans manifoldly skilled[159]—let this present, given by the Pāṇḍya prince, be bestowed upon the bard.' (231)[160]

Then Bhoja, perceiving for the very first time the marvellous conduct of Vikramārka, abandoned (his) own pride.

Then upon a time the King, roving about at night in the city of Dhārā (and) seeing a shivering Brāhman reciting as follows in a temple, stood (there):

> 'For me, indwelt by cold, sunk in the sea of anxiety as in the water of Māgha,[161] (my) split lip blowing at the extinguished fire, (my) belly emaciated by hunger, [*52*] sleep, like a despised darling, abandoning (me, hath) gone somewhere afar; night, like wealth bestowed on good folk, passeth not away.' (232)[162]

Hearing this (and) summoning him on the morrow, the King asked: 'Brāhman, how (was) the hard burden of cold borne by thee last night?' The Brāhman said:

> 'By night the knee,[163] by day the sun, at dawn and twilight the fire—thus by knee, sun, (and) fire the cold was obviated by me.' (233)

The King gave him three jars of gold (pieces). Then the poet lauds the King:

[157] Ascribed to the Jain Siddhasena in Mer. 15, 68 (Taw. 12), where it is a laudation of Vikramāditya, not of Bhoja; to Haricandra in Sad. III, liv, 4.

[158] The weighing of one's self against gold or some other valuable substance (Hindī *tulā*).

[159] Cf. Schmidt, pp. 791-792.

[160] According to Śārṅ. 565, this stanza is spoken by the comptroller of the treasury, except 'upon the bard,' which is said by Vikramārka; from the religious account-book of Vikrama in Mer. 68 (Taw. 39); to Vikrama's treasurer in Vikrama. SR xxx, 16; JR xxx, 3.

[161] The month of Māgha begins at the winter solstice.

[162] Ascribed to Mātṛgupta in Subhāṣ. 3181.

[163] I. e., by putting his head between his knees.

'By thee, sustaining me with great generosity, wealth, (and) life, Bali, Karṇa, and others (have) been released from the *karma* hidden by their own glory.' (234)[164]

The King gave him a lakh.

Upon a time the keeper of the pleasure-garden, approaching, left a stalk of sugar-cane before the King, (and) the King took it in (his) hand. Then the poet Mayūra, of account of (his) extraordinary intimacy (with Bhoja, but) reflecting in mind on the disesteem felt (toward him) by the King, said, under the guise of a sugar-cane:

'⟨Beautiful⟩ art thou, ever ⟨sweet⟩ art thou, full of ⟨flavour⟩ art thou, and, moreover, an incomparable ⟨bow⟩ of the Five-Arrowed One [Kāma, the God of Love] (art thou); O sugar-cane, all is thine, but one thing (is) lacking: that (though) ⟨cultivated⟩, thou apportionest bit by bit lack of ⟨flavour⟩; ([for, O King,] ⟨desired⟩ art thou, ever ⟨charming⟩ art thou, full of ⟨affection⟩ art thou, and, moreover, an incomparable ⟨cause⟩ of the Five-arrowed One [art thou]; all is thine, but one thing [is] lacking: that, [though] ⟨honoured⟩, thou apportionest bit by bit lack of ⟨affection⟩.' (235)

The King, knowing the poet's heart, honoured Mayūra.

Then upon a time the King, devoted to pleasure at night on the palace (roof), said, gazing at the moon:

'Since it spreadeth the sportiveness of a bit of cloud within the moon, folk call it [the moon] "the hare,"[165] (but) not so for me.'

Then a thief, entering the palace on the ground-floor, said:

'But I think the moon (hath) a body marked by minute scars of wounds from the falling of the firebrands of the sidelong glances of young (wives) agitated by parting from thy foes.' (236)[166]

Hearing that, the King said: 'Illustrious (sir), who (art) thou (that) art in the midst of (my) treasury at midnight?' He said: 'Sire, grant us immunity.' The King: 'So (be it).' Then the thief, doing obeisance to the King, told his story. The King, pleased, [*53*] gave the thief ten ten-millions of gold (pieces) and eight lordly must-elephants. Then the comptroller of the treasury writes in the religious (account) book:

'So to this thief, (his) fear of death dispelled, the King, pleased because of the preceding distich, gave ten ten-millions of gold (pieces) and eight lordly elephants with mountains destroyed by the tips of (their) tusks, (and) with buzzing bees delighted by (their) ichor.' (237)

---

[164] For Bali see note 146, and for Karṇa note 36.

[165] Instead of 'the man in the moon' the Hindus see 'the hare in the moon.'

[166] Ascribed to Harṣadeva and a thief in Subhāṣ. 1978. This stanza and the following also in Mer. 67 (Taw. 38).

Then upon a time a door-keeper, approaching, said: 'Sire, a sage with (only) a remnant of a loin-cloth is at the door.' The King: 'Let (him) enter.' Then the poet, entering, gazing on Bhoja, (and) thinking: 'To-day will there be disappearance of my poverty,' delighted, shed tears of joy. The King, looking at him, said: 'Poet, why dost thou weep?' Then said the poet: 'O King, harken to the plight of my house:

> 'Ah me! (My) sad-faced spouse, hearing on the road the loud cry, "Parched grain," carefully stopped the ears of (our) child; my expedients exhausted, thou, on the other hand, (art) the proper (one) to draw out the barb within me which made (my) eyes full of tears.' (238)

Crying, 'Śiva, Śiva! Kṛṣṇa, Kṛṣṇa!' (and) giving (him) a lakh per syllable, the King said: 'Good poet, go home quickly; thy wife was distressed (indeed).'

Then upon a time the King, utterly weary with hunting, sought the shade of a great tree. There a poet named Śāmbhavadeva, approaching, said to the King under the guise of a tree:

> 'By (thy) perfumes the winds, by the appearance of (thy) shoots the gazelles, by (thy) bark the ascetics, by (thy) flowers the bees, by (thy) fruits the birds, by (thy) shade the heat-oppressed, by (thy) trunks the must-elephants—just by thee all (are) made content; thus thou art capable of benefits to all; by Thy Majesty other trees (have their) misfortunes annulled. (239)

'And, moreover:

> 'The diction of good poets with qualities (hitherto) unknown poureth a stream of sweetness in the ears; and a jasmine-wreath enchanteth the eye, even (though its) perfume (be) not gained.' (240)[167]

The King, amazed by these two stanzas, gave a lakh per syllable.

On another occasion noble Bhoja went to a temple of Śiva to worship the Mighty Lord. Then a Brāhman said to the King in Śiva's presence: 'Sire,

> [*54*] 'Half of Śiva taken by the Foe of the Dānavas [Śiva], half, moreover, by the Mountain's Daughter [Gaurī, or Pārvatī], is thus manifest, Sire, on earth's surface in the absence of the Taker of Cities; the Ganges came to the ocean, a digit of the moon to the sky, the Lord of Serpents [Vāsuki] to the face of the world, omniscience (and) sovereignty to thee, but to me wandering beggary.' (241)[168]

The King gave a lakh per syllable.

[167] = IS 680; *Vāsavadattā*, stanza 11; also ascribed to Subandhu in Śārṅ. 145; Sūk. iv, 13.

[168] Ascribed to Śaṅkara in Śārṅ. 1529. The reference is to the androgynous aspect of Śiva, the victor over the evil deities at the Churning of the Ocean, who is adorned by the Ganges, the moon, and Vāsuki (see note 53 and stanza 84).

Then upon a time a door-keeper, approaching, said: 'Sire, a sage [169] standeth at the door.' The King: 'Let (him) enter.' Then the sage, entering, recites:

> 'As if through envy, Lord of Men, poverty quickly abandoneth him whom thy kindly glance favoureth even for an instant.' (242)

The King gave a lakh. Again the poet recites:

> 'Some (have their) hopes ⟨confused at the root⟩; some, again, (are) ⟨sharing connexion with the trunk⟩; some (have) ⟨reached the shade⟩; others ⟨bring shoots up to the fore-foot (of the tree)⟩; others carry ⟨flowers⟩ in (their) hand; then others (are) a vessel ⟨simply of perfume⟩; ([for] some [have their] hopes ⟨occupied with the Primal Cause⟩; some, again, [are] ⟨devoted to the relations of the *skandha* [metre]⟩; [170] some [have] ⟨attained to beauty [of diction]⟩; others ⟨raise up strength to exalted verse⟩; others carry ⟨gallantry⟩ in [their] hand; then others [are] a vessel of the ⟨connexion of words [with one another]⟩); but fools, alas, cannot perceive the fruit of the tendril of speech!' (243)

Hearing this, Bāṇa said:

> 'Sometimes indeed, and from the addition of ambrosia, treacle, flower-juice, honey, (and) milk, a limited flavour acquireth extreme insipidity; but in the diction of poets brilliant as the *bimba*-lip [171] of the beloved there (is) some new joy unbounded—this flavour (is) unequalled.' (244)

Then the King gave a lakh.

Then upon a time, noble Bhoja adorning the lion-throne, a door-keeper, approaching, said: 'Sire, a poet named Bhavabhūti, come from the land of Benares, standeth at the door.' The King said: 'Let (him) enter.' Then he, entering, went to the court, (and) then all the courtiers (were) pleased by his coming. And the King, perceiving Bhavabhūti, made obeisance (to him); and he, saying, 'Hail!' sat down at his [Bhoja's] bidding. Bhavabhūti said: 'Sire,

> 'Bees are not brought to honey by the flowers of the coral-tree; chickores [172] are not invited to moonlight by Him of Cold Radiance [the moon]; [173]

---

[169] V gives his name as Dharmadatta.

[170] Synonymous with Āryāgīti, a distich of $16 + 16 = 32$ syllabic instants (*mātrās*) in each verse (see C. Cappeller, *Die Gaṇachandas*, n. p., 1872, pp. 20-21; A. Weber, *Ueber die Metrik der Inder*, Berlin, 1863, pp. 289, 295, 302-307).

[171] A woman's lips are often compared to the bright-red berries of the *bimba* (Momordica Monadelpha).

[172] The large, bright-red flowers of the coral-tree (Sanskrit *pārijāta*, Erythrina Indica) are odourless. The chickore (Sanskrit *cakora*), the red-legged partridge or its close congener, Caccabis Chukor, is supposed to live only on drink from moon-beams (cf. Yule-Burnell, pp. 194-195), and its eyes are believed to turn red in the presence of poison.

[173] Reading *tuhinarucinā* with V and T instead of *tuhinarucinaś* with P.

> [*55*] attaining the quintessence of the sweetness[174] of our diction, former arrivals would be joyful (and) themselves here (be) wise; what use of requests in vain? (245)

> 'For us (there is) no palanquin nor any benefaction by adornment with armlets and the like, no lofty steed nor any retainer, not even a handsome garment; but ours (is) irreproachable knowledge delighting the mind (and) bowing the head of all the wise existing on earth's surface (and) rejoicing in understanding of (poetic) art.' (246)

Hearing this, the son of the scholar Bāṇa said: 'Knave, make no boast in the court of the Lord of Dhārā!

> '⟨An arrow⟩ the road to the heart, not even a sigh goeth forth; but what of Sarasvatī, ⟨bound at the feet⟩ of manifest pride? ([For] ⟨Bāṇa⟩ the road to the heart, not even a sigh goeth forth; but what of Sarasvatī, ⟨composed in verses⟩ of manifest pride?)' (247)

Then said Bhavabhūti, not enduring humiliation:

> 'If, to-day or to-morrow, a fellow, a composer of some verses violently dragged together, should, alas, be rivalling a poet with diction controlled, why much (talking) here in (this) evil age?[175] (That would be) a quarrel of a maker of water-jars and the Creator of the threefold world.' (248)

Again he said:

> 'If at any time the voice of Kālidāsa inciteth (one to) equality of substance[176] with my speech, sore afraid (will it be) at every ⟨step⟩ (or, at every ⟨verse⟩).' (249)

Then said Kālidāsa: 'Friend Bhavabhūti, thou art a great poet. What need (be) said on that score?

> 'This assembly of the Lord of Dhārā, adorned by great scholars, knoweth the difference between us twain, or (else) the King, like unto Śiva.' (250)

Hearing that, the King said: 'The termination of amorous dalliance (is) to be described by you both.' Bhavabhūti:

> 'The orb of the moon had an adornment of ⟨pearls⟩, (but had ⟨lost them⟩); the sky, (its) stars scattered; Love's bow had (its) quivering gone; the blue lotus closed; vanished the gentle cooing of the dove, gentled by the gentle breezes; the champak-creeper had (its) clusters motionless; after that I know not.' (251)[177]

---

[174] Lit., 'the sweetness of sweetness.'

[175] The Kali age, the last and worst of the four ages of the world, in which man now lives.

[176] Reading, with V, *arthasāmyaṁ* instead of the *adya sāmyaṁ* of P and T (with *kadācid* 'at any time' *adya* 'to-day' is meaningless here).

[177] The orb of the moon, at first adorned with pearls (the stars), alludes to the girl's face, adorned with drops of sweat; the night-sky, to her black hair, decked

[*56*] Then said Kālidāsa:

'Sweating (was) the moon's orb; dishevelled the darkness, intertwined with a burden of garlands; at first a sweet smile like expanding tufts of screw-pine;[178] ceased the wild dance of the ear-rings; part-closed the pair of blue lotuses; gone the ecstatic note of the coral; what happened after that I know not.' (252)

The King said to Kālidāsa: 'Good poet, equality of thee with Bhavabhūti must not (be) spoken of.' Bhavabhūti said: 'Sire, why dost thou forbid (it)?' The King: 'In every way thou art a poet.' Then said Bāṇa: 'O King, if Bhavabhūti (is) a poet, what (is) Kālidāsa to be called?' The King: 'Poet Bāṇa, Kālidāsa (is) not a poet, but simply some human incarnation of Pārvatī [Sarasvatī] on earth.' Then said Bhavabhūti: 'Sire, what excellence appeareth here?' The King said: 'Bhavabhūti, how much more should excellence be spoken of in Kālidāsa's verse since "a sweet smile like tufts of screw-pine" (hath been) recited!' Then said Bhavabhūti: 'Sire, thou speakest with partiality.' Then said Kālidāsa: 'Sire, let there be no discredit. Going to the temple of the Mistress of the World [Pārvatī] (and) honouring her in her (own) presence, complete clarification (here) should be made by thee in a water-jar.'

Then, surrounded by all the poet-throng, reaching the temple of the Mistress of the World, there, in her presence, giving a water-jar in Bhavabhūti's hand, and writing the two stanzas on two leaves equal (in weight), Bhoja put (them) on the balance. Then the goddess, devoted to (her) worshipper, recognising a slight elevation because of lightness on Bhavabhūti's side, (and thinking:) 'Let there be no humilation of him in the assembly,' taking juice of the white lotus from her own ear-garland with the tip of the nail of (her) left hand, cast (it) on Bhavabhūti's leaf. Then said Kālidāsa:

'Alas! my good fortune and Bhavabhūti's diction put in the balance, and lightness reflected therein, straightway for completion the divine Goddess of Speech [Sarasvatī = Pārvatī] casteth in the sweetness of the pollen of a bud of white lotus carried on her ear.' (253)

Then Bhavabhūti falls at Kālidāsa's feet and considered the King (to

with bright flowers dishevelled in dalliance; Kāma's bow, to her arching brows become motionless with exhaustion; the blue lotus, to her eyes; the dove's cooing, to her murmurs and sighs during embrace; the champak-creeper (Michelia Champaca, a sort of magnolia with very fragrant yellow blossoms), to her slender body; and its motionless clusters, to her breasts; so also in the following stanza, with the addition of coral for her lips.

[178] Pandanus Odoratissimus, a plant or small tree whose tender white leaves yield an especially delightful perfume.

be) cognisant of the difference (between them). Then the King gave the poet Bhavabhūti an hundred must-elephants.

On another occasion the King, roving about alone at night in the city of Dhārā, (and) seeing an uninhibited woman[179] going to an assignation, asked: 'Lady, who (art) thou, and where goest thou alone at midnight?' [57] Then the shrewd uninhibited woman, ascertaining (him to be) noble Bhoja roving about at night, said:

> 'Different from thee, O King, Lord of Earth, (is) He of the Odd (Number of) Arrows,[180] whose command Rudra and the rest, bear, like slaves, upon (their) head.' (254)

Then the King, pleased, taking a bracelet and an armlet from (his) mighty arm, gave (them) to her; and she went to (her) destination.

Then, going along the road (and) seeing a woman weeping alone somewhere in a house, he sent a body-guard to find out why she wept at midnight(and) what (was) her distress. Then the body-guard, returning, said: 'Sire, hear what she said (when) asked by me:

> 'This aged husband of mine (hath) taken to (his) bed; this house (hath only) remnants of posts; this (is) the time of the coming of clouds [the rainy season]; the news of (our) child (is) not good; upset because the jar of drops of carefully gathered sesamum-oil (is) broken, the mother-in-law weepeth long, seeing her daughter-in-law languid with the burden in (her) womb.' (255)

Then the Protector of Earth, an ocean of pity, gave her a lakh.

On another occasion a Brāhman dwelling in the Konkan land said, uttering 'Hail!' to the King:

> 'In the ocean of thy glory, Bhoja, heaven and earth (are) in the double hollow of a pearl-shell, arising wherefrom, methinks, (is) the pearl (which is) the orb of Him of Cold Rays [the moon].' (256)

The King gave him a lakh.

On another occasion one from the land of Kāśmīr, with (only) a remnant of a loin-cloth, seeing poets standing in the King's presence adorned with gold, rubies, (and) turban-cloths, said to the King:

> 'Our hands have not the tinkling of finest bracelets; in (our) ears no ear-rings; no pair of garments[181] with the lovely splendour of the milk of the tossing Milk-Ocean (as) an adornment; no palanquin with the brilliance of ivory poles; no steed above all exalted; (but,) O King, skill in the art of eloquence in the King's court (is) ours.' (257)

---

[179] For the 'uninhibited woman' (*svairiṇī*), who, without being a common courtesan, goes of her own accord to assignations with her lover, see Schmidt, pp. 208-209.

[180] I. e., Kāma, the God of Love, who has five arrows.

[181] I. e., an outer and an under garment.

Then the King gave him a lakh.

On another occasion the King, seeing the orb of the moon at night, described the spot within it:

> 'Some have supposed (it to be) a brand; others have thought (it to be) ocean's mud;[182] some have called (it) a dappled antelope; others wished (to see in it) earth's shadow.'

[*58*] Thus writing the first half, the King gave (it) into Kālidāsa's hand. Then at that very instant the poet writes the second half:

> 'What is always seen in the moon black as a chip of split sapphire we declare (to be) thick, densest darkness drunk in the night (and) remaining in (his)[183] belly.' (258)

The King gave a lakh per syllable for the second half. Then the King, perceiving the sequence of Kālidāsa's poesy, astonished, again said: 'Friend, describe the moon without a spot.' Then the poet recites:

> 'The pool for Lakṣmī's sport, the white mansion of Rati [the wife of the God of Love], the mirror of the brides of the (eight) quarters (of the compass), a flower of the dark creeper,[184] the parasol of the God of Love conquering the triple world, the smile of Hara [Śiva] made into a ball, the white lotus of the river of the gods [the celestial Ganges], He with the Deer for His Ensign, the pond of the nectar of moonlight, the white spouse of the galaxy of stars, doth conquer.' (259)

Again the King gave a lakh per syllable.

Upon a time a lute-poet, come from a far country, said:

> 'I (am) no wayfarer versed in philosophy (and) grammar, not learned in poetic composition; I know not marvellous skill in arrangement of manifold diction; (but) even so, some goddess, a darling daughter of Viriñci [Brahmā], abiding in my mouth, speaketh some soft, sweet, uninterrupted tone of the lute in (my) hand.' (260)

The King gave him a lakh. Bāṇa, hearing his very charming composition, said: 'Sire,

> 'Those knowing (only figurative) allusions do not even touch the highest sweetness as (they do not touch) a Caṇḍāla woman;[185] those intoxicated (only) with (poetic) sentiments do not see proficiency (in literary) style as (they do not see) a maiden of good family; a union of proficiency (and)

---

[182] I. e., as apparently arising from the ocean.

[183] The moon is masculine in Sanskrit.

[184] *Śyāmālatā*, a creeping plant variously identified with the Echites Frutescens, Hemidesmus Indicus, or Ichnocarpus Frutescens.

[185] An outcaste of the lowest and most despised of the mixed tribes, born of a Brāhman mother by a Śūdra father.

6

sweetness, a friend of the perfume of musk (and) camphor, becometh an elixir for the ear of some fortunate one.' (261)[186]

On another occasion the King said to Sītā in the morning: 'Lady, describe the dawn.' Sītā said:

'The stout stars (became) exceeding thin like good folk in the Kali (Age);[187] everywhere the sky became clear like an ascetic's mind; darkness goeth like an evil man from the thought of the good; and night swift departeth like the fortune of them that strive not.' (262)[188]

[*59*] Giving a lakh, the King said to Kālidāsa: 'Friend, good poet, do thou also describe the dawn.' Kālidāsa:

'Tawny became the stars like quicksilver eating gold; the moon's lustre (is) gone like a wise man in a session of villagers; in an instant the stars (have) waned like princes not devoted to diligence; the lamps shine not like the qualities of them bereft of wealth.' (263)[189]

The King gave him a lakh per syllable.

On another occasion a door-keeper, approaching, said: 'Sire, a garland-maker's wife standeth at the door.' The King: 'Let (her) enter.' Then she, entering and making obeisance, recites:

'Thy glory, resplendent as the streams of rays of the moon-banner gleaming on the top of Hara's [Śiva's] crest, is sung by one with a sweet lute sounding with the fruit of the trumpet-gourd kissing the cluster of (her) high, firm breasts (and) with the glancing brow of the world of the gods.' (264)

The King, saying: 'Ah, great sequence of words!' gave her a lakh per syllable.

On another occasion the King, roving about in the city of Dhārā by night, saw in some one's house a woman engrossed with a pestle. Regarding her, young, with a face like the full moon, (and) with very delicate limbs, the King said to the pestle in her hand: 'O pestle, not even by the touch of the twigs of this (lady's) hand was there a bud in thee; so in every way thou (art) only wood.' Then the King recited one verse:

'Since, O pestle, a bud (was) not born of thee at that instant.'

Then on the morrow, perceiving Kālidāsa come to the court, (and)

[186] For 'figurative allusions' (*dhvani*), 'sweetness' (*mādhurī, mādhurya*), and 'poetic sentiment' (*rasa*) see Regnaud, pp. 83-106, 237-290, 267-316.

[187] See note 175.

[188] Ascribed to a group of Bhoja's poets in Śārṅ. 2217; cf. IS 6174.

[189] Ascribed to a group of Bhoja's poets in Śārṅ. 3717. V and T read *vinayarahitānām* 'bereft of good breeding' instead of the *draviṇarahitānām* 'bereft of wealth' of P.

reciting: 'Since, O pestle, a bud (was) not born of thee at that instant,' the King said: 'Good poet, do thou recite three verses.' Then said Kālidāsa:

> 'This (is) known in the world, thou art now only wood, and that, indeed, is true; thou hast grown up in the forest, since, O pestle, a bud (was) not born of thee at that instant even in this festival of contact with the hand of one with eyes (like) a new blue lotus.' (265)

Then the King gave (him) a lakh per syllable for the three verses.

[*60*] On another occasion, having long indulged in water-sport, the King sat, utterly weary, in the shade of a fig-tree on its bank. There a poet, approaching, said:

> 'Noble Lord Bhoja, dexterous in protecting the earth! The ruler of the southern land [the Deccan],[190] seeing for an instant the sky hidden by the burden of dust of Thy Majesty's armies, (hath) fled without hestitation, without shame, without followers, without kinsfolk, without friends, without wife, without children, without younger brother, without gold. (266)

'And, moreover:

> 'The (eight) quarters (of the sky, when) looked upon, (are) black with the dust arising from the night of Thy Majesty's broad armies glittering with exceeding eagerness (for the fray), with cranes, (their) festivals unexpectedly held (though) determined upon at (Lake) Mānasa,[191] with flocks of peafowl with unexpected skilful dances.' (267)

Then the King gave (him) two lakhs. At that time, perceiving a crow cawing on a branch and a koel[192] singing on another branch, a poet named Devajaya said:

> 'Not pleasing ⟨feet⟩, not even a ⟨charming beak⟩, not a ⟨song⟩ worth speaking of, not a ⟨gait gracefully quick⟩, not ⟨possession of a white wing⟩ (are) thine, foolish crow ([for] not pleasing ⟨verses⟩, not even an ⟨ingenious mouth⟩, not a ⟨word⟩ worth speaking of, not a ⟨manner agreeably apt⟩, not a ⟨pure adherence⟩ [are] thine). Lifting up quite frivolously in this place a voice full of harsh cawing, art thou not ashamed, making a show of unseemly learning?' (268)[193]

Then a rival poet named Hariśarman, considering this (poem) composed under the guise of a crow by the poet Devajaya (to be) railing at himself, said angrily (and) filled with envy:

[190] Cf. stanza 6.
[191] See note 70.
[192] Sanskrit *kokila, pika,* the Indian cuckoo, which in India enjoys the same esteem for its song that the nightingale does in England.
[193] Ascribed to Vālmīki in Subhāṣ. 764; anonymous in Sūk. xvii, 9.

'By whom is a black (bird) with wings of like colour, associated with koels, named a crow if he himself speak not?' (269)

Then the King, knowing the enmity of Hariśarman and Devajaya, one for the other, made friendship (between them) by mutual embraces and the like, and by the gifts of garments, adornments, and so forth.

On another occasion the King, mounting (his) vehicle, going along the road, (and) seeing a certain treasure of asceticism,[194] said to him: 'The sight of (folk) like Your Honours (is) dependent on Fate. Where (is) Your Honours' abode, or who are asked (by Your Honours) for food?' Then, hearing the King's voice, the treasure of asceticism said:

'The fruit of trees to be taken at pleasure (and) unwearyingly in every forest; cool, sweet water of pure streams in every place; [*61*] a bed, soft to the touch, made of the shoots of most delightful creepers—even so the poor bear affliction at the door of the rich. (270)[195]

'O King, we ask nothing and we take nothing.' The King, pleased, does (him) obseisance.

Then one come from the north country said 'Hail!' to the King; and the King asks him: 'Sage, where (is) thine abode?' The sage said:

'Where water despiseth ambrosia, and the lowest born the lords of the gods, and stones the wishing-gem—there (is) our abode, O King.' (271)

Then, giving (him) a lakh, the King said: 'What special news in the land of Benares?' He said: 'Sire, some marvellous news (is) heard there now by the mouth of folk, that the gods (are) wretched because of distress.' The King: 'Whence, sage, (is) the distress of the gods?' And he said:

'The recent news, Bhoja, is that the gods (have their) minds distraught, (asking:) "Where to-day (is) our abode, the Gold Mountain [Meru],[196] given (away) by Bhoja?"' (272)

Then, pleased by the intriguing saying, the King again gave him a lakh.

Then said a door-keeper: 'Sire, a sage devoted to chastity (and) come from Śrīśaila[197] is at the door.' The King said: 'Let (him)

[194] The Bengali recension calls him Viśvāvasu.

[195] = IS 4368; also in *Prabodhacandrodaya* iv, 9; ascribed to Kṛṣṇamiśra in Sūk. cxxviii, 3.

[196] A fabled mountain in the centre of the earth, on which is Svarga (Indra's heaven), containing the cities of the gods and the habitations of celestial spirits.

[197] Also called Śrīparvata, the Palni Hills in Madura (Madras).

enter.' Then the chaste Brāhman,[198] approaching, says: 'Live long!' The King asks him: 'Brāhman, what, in sooth, (is) thy vow, suitable, even in youth, for the Kali Age?[199] Thou art emaciated by fasting day after day. What Brāhman's daughter shall I have given to thee if thou wilt assent to the duties of a householder?' The chaste Brāhman said: 'Sire, thou (art) master. What (is) impossible for thee?

> 'Gazelles (their) friends; (their) house a mountain-cave; (their) dear spouse quietism; (their) sustenance by the fruits of forest-creepers; (their) best raiment the bark of trees—this (is) bliss for them (whose) minds (are) submerged in the ambrosia-flood of meditation on the That; [200] we have no longing even for the release [201] (vouchsafed) to them (that) concentrate on him whose crest (is) a digit of the moon [202] [Śiva].' (273)

The King, arising, falls at (his) feet and said: 'Brāhman, what should I do?' He said: 'Sire, we long to go to Benares; so arrange accordingly. Send to Benares with (their) wives all those most excellent scholars who (are) at thine abode. Then I, delighted with (their) comradeship, shall go to Benares.' So the King did.

Then all the most excellent scholars set forth at his bidding; Kālidāsa alone went not. [*62*] Then said the King to Kālidāsa: 'Good poet, why hast thou not gone?' Then said Kālidāsa to the King: 'Sire, thou art omniscient.

> 'Those sages go to (holy) bathing-places who from Śambhu [Śiva] (are) afar; he in whose heart the Lord of Gaurī [Śiva] (dwelleth), Bhoja, (is) the best (holy) bathing-place.' (274)

Then upon a time, the sages gone to Benares, the King asked Kālidāsa in the assembly: 'Kālidāsa, hath not somewhat (been) heard by thee to-day?' He said:

> 'On Meru, in the caves of Mandara, on Himālaya's summit, on Mount Mahendra, on Kailāsa's rocky slabs, even on Malaya's slopes, yea, on Mount Sahya, in each one, Bhoja, hath thy glory many times (been) heard by me loud-sung by hosts of bards in (their) wanderings on Lokāloka.' (275)[203]

---

[198] *Brahmacārin*, an unmarried Brāhman student in the first of the four stages of the ideal Indian life, the other three being those of the householder (*gṛhastha*), the forest-hermit (*vānaprastha*), and the ascetic or pious mendicant (*yati*).

[199] See note 175.

[200] Brahmā; cf. the Vedāntic phrase, *Tat tvam asi* 'That [the All-Soul, Brahmā] art thou.'

[201] I. e., from reincarnation, with absorption into the Infinite and annihilation of all personal individuality.

[202] The Hindus divide the moon into sixteen digits (*kalā*).

[203] Mandara, a mountain in Bhāgalpur (Bengal), supposed to have been the churning-stick employed by the gods and demons at the Churning of the Ocean; Mahendra, one of the seven mountain-ranges of India in Ganjam (Madras Presi-

Then the King, amazed, gave (him) a lakh per syllable.

Then upon a time, knowing (that) the throng of sages (had) gone and (that) Kālidāsa (was) incessantly greedy for courtesans, the King reflected: 'Alas! Bāṇa, Mayūra, and the others have done my bidding, and this (Kālidāsa), through lust for courtesans, heedeth not my bidding. What do we do?' Then the King looked at Kālidāsa contemptuously. Then Kālidāsa, knowing within himself the King's contempt, going to the land of Ballāla,[204] (and) reaching the lord of that land, said: 'Sire, because of the contempt of Bhoja, Lord of Mālava, I, a poet named Kālidāsa, (have) reached thy land.' Then the King, seating him on (his) own throne, said: 'Good poet, thy greatness (hath been) agreed upon an hundred times by scholars come hither from Bhoja's court. Good poet, they say thou (art) Sarasvatī. Then recite somewhat.' Then said Kālidāsa:

> 'Lord Ballāla, a Kirāta woman,[205] roaming in the city of thy foes (and) taking scattered gems, (her) limbs agitated through fear of coals of very broad catechu, throwing thereover a quantity of sandal, (her) eyes become (like) buds, (and) blowing (the supposed fire), hath fear of smoke because of the swarms of bees following (her) on account of the perfume of (her) breath.' (276)

Then (the King) gave him a lakh per syllable.

Then upon a time Ballālarāja asked Kālidāsa: 'Good poet, describe the city of Ekaśilā.'[206] Then said the poet:

> [63] 'In every street, at every step in the city of Ekaśilā youths (are) fettered, without fault (on their part), by the side-long, pretextful glances of gazelle-eyed (damsels).' (277)

---

dency); Kailāsa, a mountain of the Himālayas, north of Lake Mānasa (see notes 54, 70); Malaya, the mountain-range on the east of Malabar; Sahya, another of the seven mountain-ranges, in the north-west of the Deccan; Lokāloka ('World and Not-World'), 'a mythical belt or circle of mountains surrounding the outermost of the seven seas and dividing the visible world from the region of darkness (as the sun is within this wall of darkness they are light on one side and dark on the other)' (M. Monier-Williams, *Sanskṛit-English Dictionary*, new ed., Oxford, 1899, p. 907b).

[204] Probably Ballāḷa II (Vīra-Ballāḷa, Tribhuvanamalla, or Bhujabala-Vīra-Gaṅga) of the Hoysaḷa dynasty, ruling (1173-1224) at Dvārāvatipura or Dvārasamudra (the modern Halebīd in Mysore); see Duff, pp. 160, etc. T reads *Allāḷa*.

[205] The Kirātas were a degraded mountain-folk living by the chase (cf. note 44); their women were the Royal chowry-bearers. In her simplicity this woman thinks that the flashing gems are flames, and that the swarms of bees are smoke.

[206] Apparently Ballāḷa's capital, and, if so, an alternative name ('One-Rock [City]') for Dvārāvatipura ('City with [Many] Gates').

And again he gave (him) a lakh per syllable; and again the poet recites:

'Youths (are) smitten by the arrows of the Bodiless One [the God of Love], (which are) the glances askant of (damsels with) eyes long (as) lotus-leaves here assembled in pools ocean-long.' (278)

And again Prince Ballāla gave (him) a lakh; so Kālidāsa remained right there.

Meanwhile in the city of Dhārā a door-keeper, coming to Bhoja, said: 'Sire, a most excellent scholar named Māgha, arrived from the land of Gurjara [Gujarat], sitteth outside the city, and his wife (hath been) sent by him to the King's door.' The King said: 'Let her enter.' Then Māgha's wife (was) permitted to enter; she put a letter in the King's hand; the King, taking it, reads:

'Deprived of beauty (is) the cluster of white lotuses, beauteous the group of day-lotuses; the owl forsaketh joy; happy (is) the *cakravāka*; to (his) rising goeth he of not-cold rays [the sun], to (his) setting he of chill beams [the moon]; Oh, diverse (is) the fruition of (those) stricken by evil Fate!' (279)[207]

The King, hearing this marvellous description of dawn (and) giving three lakhs, said to Māgha's wife: 'Mother, this is given for food. On the morrow, going to the scholar Māgha (and) doing (him) obeisance, I shall fulfil (his) wishes.' Then she, going with it (and) hearing from the mouth of beggars her husband's virtues, brilliant (as) the rays of the autumnal moon, gave them all the wealth given by Bhoja. Then, reaching her husband, the scholar Māgha, she said: 'Husband, I (have been) much honoured by King Bhoja; (but,) hearing thy virtues, I have given all the wealth to beggars.' Māgha said: 'Well done, lady; but those beggars are coming along (with thee); what should (be) given them?' Then a beggar, knowing the scholar Māgha (to have only) a remnant of a garment, said:

'This, in sooth, (is) thy highest glory, cloud, that thou art empty comforting a multitude of mountains burned by the sun's heat and forests distressed by unrestrained woodland fires, and filling divers hundreds of rivers, both female and male.' (280)[208]

[*64*] Māgha, hearing this, said to his wife: 'Lady,

[207] = Mer. 86 (Taw. 50). The male and female *cakravākas, cakras, kokas*, Brahminy ducks or ruddy geese (Anas Casarca), are supposed to be separated, mourning, from each other all the night, being united only during the day (see Yule-Burnell, p. 112).

[208] = IS 1059 (Sad. IV, lxi, 1).

'Wealth is not, and despair releaseth me not; my wayward mind hath delight in giving; and begging (is) degrading; and in self-murder (is) sin. O life, depart of thyself! Why lamentation? (281)[209]

'The burning of the fire of poverty (is) quenched by the water of gratification; by what is the inward fire of a beggar's stricken hope quenched?' (282)[210]

So then all the beggars, perceiving the plight of the scholar Māgha, went to (their) destinations. Then, those beggars gone to (their) destinations, Māgha said:

'Depart, depart, O life, the beggars become useless; and (I) must follow. Where (will) such wealth (as) this (be) again?' (283)

Thus lamenting, the scholar Māgha went to the Other World. Then Māgha's wife, (her) lord gone to the Other World, said:

'The scholar Māgha, whose house kings always frequented like slaves, dieth together with his spouse.' (284)

Then the King, knowing (that) Māgha (was) dead, went there silently by night, surrounded by an hundred sages from his city. Then Māgha's wife, seeing the King, said: 'O King, since the most excellent scholar, having reached thy land, hath gone to the Other World, then (what) remaineth to be done for him must be done[211] aright by Thy Majesty.' Then, taking the dead Māgha to the banks of the Narmadā, the King performed the rite (of cremation) according to the ritual prescribed. And then Māgha's wife entered the fire, and Bhoja did all for them like a son.

Then, Māgha gone to heaven, the King, filled with sorrow especially because of separation from Kālidāsa and because of the scholars' residence abroad, day by day became thin as the moon's dark half. Then the ministers in assembly reflected: 'Kālidāsa dwelleth in Ballāla's land; the King in that city will be happy.' By the ministers thus considering, writing somewhat in a letter and giving that letter into the hand of a minister, it was sent. Reaching Kālidāsa in the course of time, bowing (before him, and saying:) 'I (am) sent by the King's ministers,' (the minister) gave (him) that letter. Then Kālidāsa reads it:

'It existeth not (at all, or) it existeth not for long; if it doth exist for long, (it is) disappointing in result; the anger of good folk (is) like the affection of the base. (285)

---

[209] = Śārṅ. 407; stanzas 281-283 = Mer. 87 (Taw. 51).

[210] = stanza 103 (there spoken by Bāṇa); ascribed to Māgha also in Mer. 87 (Taw. 51) and Śārṅ. 406.

[211] Reading *karaṇīyaṁ* with V instead of *ārādhanīyaṁ* with P and T.

[*65*] 'O young koel, long remaining playfully on the mango-tree, art thou not ashamed, leaving it to-day, (to be) wandering about on other trees? (286)

'O cuckoo, consider whether thy song would be as lovely either on the catechu or the palas-tree [212] as on the mango-tree.' (287)

Then Kālidāsa, taking leave of the Prince at dawn (and) coming to the land of Mālava, stood in the King's pleasure-garden. And the King, knowing (that he had) gone there, himself going with a great retinue (and) fetching him, showed (him) honour. And then, the circle of sages gradually come together, Bhoja's assembly shone as aforetime.

Then a door-keeper, approaching Bhoja adorning the lion-throne, (and) doing obeisance, said: 'Sire, a sage coming from the land of Jālandhara [213] sitteth at the door.' The King said: 'Let (him) enter.' And come to the court (and) seeing the King in such state (and) lordly poets, Kālidāsa and the rest, honourable in the world, the sage was, as it were, tongue-tied. Naught whatsoever comes from his mouth in the court. Then said the King: 'Sage, recite somewhat.' He said:

'For fear of burning (her) throat with sour gruel, Sarasvatī (is) departed from my mouth; wherefore, O (thou whose) hand (is) intent on grasping the hair of the fortune of (thy) foes, poesy is not mine.' (288) [214]

The King gave him an hundred buffalo-cows.

On another occasion the King, filled with eagerness, said to Sītā: 'Lady, invoke Love.' Sītā said:

'Homage to Love, that cause of joy to the world, whose inherent fruit (is folk) like thee, King Bhoja!' (289) [215]

Delighted, the King gave her a pearl necklace.

Then the King, looking at a courtesan chowry-bearer, said to Kālidāsa: 'Good poet, describe this courtesan.' Looking at her, Kālidāsa said:

'The burden of (her) breasts feareth the burden of (her) hair; the burden of (her) hair, the burden of (her) breasts; (her) hips, the burden of (her) hair and breasts—what reason for amazement (is) this, moon-faced one?' (290)

---

[212] Sanskrit *palāśa*, Butea Frondosa or dhak-tree, with beautiful large red flowers, their ground-colour deep-red, shaded with orange and silvery down.

[213] A division of the Pañjāb. Mer. 102 (Taw. 62) names the sage Dhanapāla.

[214] = Mer. 102 (Taw. 62).

[215] Reading, with R. Pischel (*Festgruss an Otto von Böhtlingk*, Stuttgart, 1888, p. 94), *bhavādṛśāḥ* instead of the *bhavādṛśām* of the printed editions. Śārṅ. 511 assigns this strophe to the daughter of Sarasvatīkuṭumba (really of Amṛtadatta, a court-poet of Shihāb-ad-Dīn [1352-1370]).

[*66*] Delighted, Bhoja himself recites:

> '(Her) pair of feet are in terror of (her) face; (her) lips and row of teeth, of (her) voice; (her) pair of breasts, of (her) hair; and (her) pair of eyes, of (her) waist.' (291)

On another occasion King Bhoja, roving about alone in the city of Dhārā (and) coming to the house of a most excellent Brāhman, saw there a woman, devoted to (her) husband, holding (her) spouse lying in (her) lap. Then (her) child, rousing up from sleep, went near the flame; and, she, wholly devoted to (her) duty to (her) husband, did not arouse her husband, and did not then seize the child falling into the fire. And observing the marvel, the King stood (still). Then she, wholly devoted to (her) duty to (her) husband, besought the fire: 'Lord of Sacrifice [Agni], beholding all actions, thou knowest all duties; thou knowest (that) I (am) utterly devoted to (my) duty to (my) husband and (am) not seizing (my) child; so, receiving my child, burn (him) not!' Then the child, entering the Lord of Sacrifice and taking him by the hand, remained right there for the space of half a *ghaṭikā* [twelve minutes]. Then the child wept not and (was) of a glad countenance; and she ascended to (profound religious) meditation. Then, (her) husband spontaneously rousing up, she straightway seized the child. And, filled with amazement at beholding that extreme (devotion to) duty, the King said: 'Ah, whose fortune is equal to mine, since such pure women dwell in my city?' Then on the morrow, going to the court (and) seated on the lion-throne, the King said to Kālidāsa: 'Good poet, a great marvel hath been seen by me yesternight.' So saying, the King recites:

> 'The fire cool (as) sandalwood unguent.'

Then Kālidāsa strightway recites three verses:

> 'Seeing (her) child falling into the fire, devoted to (her) husband, she woke (her) husband not; so, because of the weightiness of (her) love for her husband, became the fire cool (as) sandalwood unguent.' (292)

And the King, perceiving his own implication, astonished (and) embracing him, fell at (his) feet.

On a time in the warm season the King, burned by the hot heat, roving about in the harem, not indulging in embraces and so forth, (but) enjoying with them the courtesies of elegant conversation and the like, slept right there. Then, rising on the morrow (and) entering the court, the King recites, out of eagerness:

> 'By the tidings of the coming of the winds at a time empty, (or) awakening, (or) even far advanced.' [216]

---

[216] I. e., in the night, at dawn, or late in the day.

[*67*] Bhavabhūti said:

> 'With the wind from (her) mouth the serpent(-mother) showed (her) hungry child her own hissing by the tidings of the coming of the winds at a time empty, (or) awakening, (or) even far advanced.' (293)

The King said: 'A relevant folk-saying, Bhavabhūti!' Then with the corner of (his) eye the King sees Kālidāsa; then he (Kālidāsa) said:

> 'Even with (their) eyes gallants experienced new embracements in women by the tidings of the coming of the winds at a time empty, (or) awakening, (or) even far advanced.' (294)

Then, delighted (and) knowing his own implication, the King honoured Kālidāsa especially.

On another occasion the King, mastered by the chase (and) utterly oppressed (by fatigue), sat at the foot of a thick-shaded rose-apple tree on the shore of a large pond. The King lying there, all the rose-apple fruits (were) shaken by many monkeys up on the rose-apple tree. Seeing them noisily falling, staying there for the space of a *ghaṭikā,* laying aside (his) weariness, arising, (and) mounting (his) horse, he departed. Then in the court the King, imitating the unprecedented sound of the falling of the fruits shaken by the monkeys, spoke a verse-capping: 'Guluguggulugugguluguggulu.' Then said Kālidāsa:

> 'In the clear water, from boughs shaken by monkeys, fall the ripe rose-apple fruits guluguggulugugguluguggulu.' (295)

The King, delighted, said: 'Good poet, how knowest thou a deep secret, even unseen? Clearly thou art Śāradā [Sarasvatī].' So speaking, he fell at (Kālidāsa's) feet again (and) again.

On a time the King, roving about in disguise in the city of Dhārā, coming at midday to the house of an aged Brāhman, stood there. Then the aged Brāhman, making the All-God (sacrifice),[217] taking the oblations for the crows, going out of (his) house, (and) scattering (it) on the ground purified with water, called a crow. There the crows gathered at the clapping of (his) hands and the sound of 'Ha! ha!' Then a crow cawed loudly. Hearing that, his young wife, laying (her) hand on her breast, as if frightened, wailed: 'O mother!' [*68*] Then the

[217] An offering to the All-Gods, 'a factitious sacrificial group meant to represent all the gods in order that none should be excluded in laudations intended to be addressed to all' (Macdonell, p. 130). The oblation must be cast by the householder at morning and at evening on the ground outside the house for dogs, birds, and dog-eating men, and is connected with the cult of the dead (Hopkins, pp. 172-173; *Mahābhārata* III, ii, 59; XIII, xcvii, 23).

Brāhman said: 'Dear one of good character, why art thou afraid?' She said: 'Husband, hearing harsh sounds (is) unendurable for wives like me, devoted to their spouses.' The Brāhman said: 'Be it even so, thou of good character!' Then the King, seeing all that behaviour, reflected: 'Alack! assuredly this young (woman is) of bad character since she is plainly afraid and herself tells of (her) devotion to her husband; assuredly she, unafraid, is doing an exceedingly terrible deed at night.' Thus reflecting, the King, hidden, took his stand at night right there. Then at midnight, (her) husband asleep, she went to the bank of the Narmadā, having a courtesan carry a basket of meat. The King, concealing himself, followed. Then, reaching the Narmadā, giving the meat to the alligators gathered there, (and) crossing the river, she took her pleasure with her paramour impaled on the farther bank.[218] Seeing that behaviour, the King, returning home (and) on the morrow seeing Kālidāsa in the court, said: 'Harken, good poet,

> 'By day afraid of the cawing of crows,'

Then said Kālidāsa:

> 'By night she crosseth the Narmadā;'

Then, delighted, the King said again:

> 'There in the water are alligators;'

The poet said:

> 'The fair (lady) herself knoweth (their) weakness.' (296)

Then the King falls at Kālidāsa's feet.

Upon a time the King, roving about in the city of Dhārā (and) seeing in the street of the courtesans a fair (girl) wholly absorbed in playing ball (and) with (her) ear-ring fallen because of the quickness of the uneven movements of (her) feet therein, said in the court: 'Let the poets describe the ball.' Then said Bhavabhūti:

> 'Surely, O ball, thy heart (is) known as if longing for union with the wanton's lips; (though) struck by the girl's lotus-hand (and) falling again and again, once more thou boundest upward.' (297)

[*69*] Then said Vararuci:

> 'Though one, this ball appeareth as three: red, red from the redness of the damsel's palm;[219] white, white from the rays of the nails of her feet on the ground; blue, blue from the light of (her) eyes in the air.' (298)[220]

---

[218] For impalement, especially for robbery, see Jolly, *Recht*, pp. 125-127, 130.

[219] Indian women dye their palms with henna.

[220] Reading, with V, *svaḥsthaḥ* (cf. *khasthaḥ* in T) instead of the *svasthaḥ* 'in (its) natural state' of P. The stanza is ascribed to Bhāravi in Sūk. lxvi, 8.

Then said Kālidāsa:

> '"Oh, the ball with the shape of (her) breast is repeatedly struck in anger by (her) hand," even thus (thinking), the lotus, fearful of the aspect of (her) eyes, hath fallen at (her) feet for (to gain) the woman's graciousness.' (299)

Then the King, delighted, gave the three a lakh per syllable, and especially did he honour Kālidāsa, the knower of the unseen fall of the flowers in (her) ear-ring.

Then upon a time the King, intent on looking at paintings (and) seeing the Great Serpent [221] painted, said: 'Well painted!' Then a poet named Śivaśarman praises the King under the guise of a serpent:

> 'There are many snakes intent (solely) on eating frogs; just this one serpent (is) capable of bearing the earth.' (300) [222]

Then the King, knowing his idea, gave him a lakh.

Upon a time, the winter-season come, the King, honouring a blazing fire-vessel,[223] said to Kālidāsa: 'Good poet, describe the fire-vessel.' Then said the good poet:

> 'As a poet's mind (hath) ⟨many inferences⟩, it (hath) ⟨much iron⟩, as the time of dawn (hath) ⟨happily united *cakras*⟩,[224] it (hath) ⟨well-joined wheels⟩; as the form of Hara [Śiva] shineth ⟨laughing⟩, possessed of ⟨the moon, Umā [Pārvatī], and fire⟩,[225] the ⟨fire-vessel⟩ shineth, possessed of ⟨fire without smoke⟩.' (301)

The King gave (him) a lakh per syllable.

Upon a time in the harem King Bhoja saw his four wives worth enjoying and equal in qualities. Seeing four qualities in them, the King meditated on the minus or the plus in those qualities—in Padmavatī, the daughter of the Lord of Kuntala,[226] (her) post-menstrual bath; in Candramukhī, the daughter [227] of the King of Añga [Bengal], the arrival of (her) turn (for the King's visit); in her named Kamalā, the gaining (of such turn) by victory in the game of dice; and in his chief queen, Līlādevī, (her) invitation (for him to come to her) by

[221] The Cosmic Serpent Śeṣa.

[222] *Dharaṇīdhara* 'earth-bearing' may also mean 'King,' and is thus an obvious allusion to Bhoja.

[223] For the worship of Agni, the Fire-God.

[224] See note 207.

[225] See note 53.

[226] In the Bellary District (Madras Presidency).

[227] As V's commentary rightly says, we should probably read *bhaginyāṁ* 'sister' instead of *putryāṁ* 'daughter' to conform with the *svasur* of stanza 302.

sending a (female) messenger (to him). There the King of Kings, noble Bhoja, in all things the receptacle of consideration, through indecision (as to their) merits because of (their) equal qualities, reflecting for two (or) three *ghaṭikās*,[228] [*70*] went to sleep. And arising on the morrow (and) performing (his) daily rites, he went to the court. And there adorning the lion-throne (and) seeing Kālidāsa, the ornament of all the circle of learned poets, noble Bhoja, saying: 'Good poet, hear this *samasyā*, (its) fourth verse minus three letters,'[229] recites:

> 'With mind confused by indecision, two (or) three *nāḍikās* (were) passed.'

So reciting, the King said to Kālidāsa: 'Good poet, fill this *samasyā*.' Then Kālidāsa, seeing (Bhoja's) mind as a myrobalan in the palm of (his) hand,[230] recites the *samasyā* triply characterised by a verse with three letters more: 'Sire,

> 'The daughter of the Lord of Kuntala hath bathed; the turn of the sister of the King of Aṅga (is come); this night (hath been) won by Kamalā at dice; now the Queen must be appeased—by the Lord [Bhoja], thus meditating on the preponderance of justice as to the qualifications of (each of these) fair (women) in (his) harem, with mind confused by indecision, two (or) three *nāḍikās* (were) passed.' (302)

Then the King fell at the feet of Kālidāsa, knowing his own (Bhoja's) mind, and the circle of poets were astonished.

Upon a time the King, roving about in the city of Dhārā, somewhere seeing a woman with a face (like) the full moon coming towards (him) carrying a full (water-)jar, and hearing a sound in the water of that jar, thinking: 'Surely in clinging to her neck, this jar murmurs, as it were, love's murmur,' said in the court to Kālidāsa: 'The murmur (is) love's murmur.' The poet said:

> '(In the jar,) ⟨burnt, with a good spout, red⟩, mounted on (her) hip, (and) clinging to the woman's beauteous neck, the murmur (is) love's murmur (for [O woman] ⟨subtle,[231] fair of face, [and] enamoured⟩, [thy] murmur [is] love's murmur).' (303)

---

[228] Forty-eight or seventy-two minutes; *ghaṭikā* is synonymous with *nāḍikā* in the stanza immediately following.

[229] The 'three letters' (*akṣara*, also meaning 'syllable') are *d*(*e*)*v*(*e*)*n*(*ā*)- in stanza 302, verse 4, since a Sanskrit 'syllable' is expressed only by the character ('letter') for a consonant or group of consonants, the vowel or diphthong following merely being implied (if for *a*) or (if for a diphthong or a vowel other than *a*) being indicated by a subordinate sign attached to the consonant or group of consonants. For the *samasyā* see note 94.

[230] See note 31. The stanza is anonymous in Sad. II, lxxxi, 2.

[231] For the *vidagdhā* 'subtle woman' see Schmidt, pp. 274-275.

Then the King, pleased, gave (him) a lakh per syllable and did (him) obeisance.

Upon a time a stone fragment with letters somewhat mutilated (was) seen by fishermen in a great pool in the Narmadā. And they thought: 'This here seemeth (to be) something written, as it were; surely this should (be) taken to the King.' Considering thus, it (was) brought to the King's seat. Hearing that, Bhoja said: 'Aforetime the glorious Rāmāyaṇa (was) made by His Honour Hanuman, (and) the tradition is that it (was) thrown into this pool.'[232] Then, (with the thought:) 'What (is) this written? By all means it should (be) studied (and) knowledge of the inscription gained,' deciphering the letters by the test of lac, he reads (them). Then two verses (were) taken in sequence:

> 'Oh, unequal in sooth among folk becometh the ripening of deeds done aforetime!'

[*71*] Then said King Bhoja: 'Let the first half of this be told.' Then said Bhavabhūti:

> 'Where now (is) the spotless race of the Long-Eyed One [Sitā]? Where now the refusal to consort with the Night-Goer [Rāvaṇa]? Oh, unequal in sooth among folk becometh the ripening of deeds done aforetime!' (304)

Then Bhoja, deeming a cacophony there, read that same first half otherwise:

> 'Where (is) Janaka's daughter [Sītā]? Where Rāma's wife [Sītā]? And where the dwelling of the Ten-Necked One [Rāvaṇa] in (his) palace? Oh, unequal in sooth among folk becometh the ripening of deeds done aforetime!' (305)

Then said Bhoja to Kālidāsa: 'Good poet, do thou read the poet's mind!' He [Kālidāsa] said:

> 'O Śiva, Śiva! The heads that shone on Śiva's head (now) roll at the vulture's feet. Oh, unequal in sooth among folk becometh the ripening of deeds done aforetime!' (306)[233]

---

[232] I. e., the *Hanumannāṭaka* or *Mahānāṭaka* (before 850), ascribed to the Monkey-God Hanuman, who is said to have thrown it into the Narmadā to spare the feelings of Vālmīki, the traditional author of the *Rāmāyaṇa* (see Wilson, ii, 372-373; Winternitz, iii, 242-245; Konow, pp. 88-90). In his commentary on the recension of Dāmodara (cf. above, stanza 220), Mohanadāsa makes him, not Kālidāsa, reconstruct the fragments. Madhusūdana's Bengali recension, on the other hand, ascribes the discovery of the tablets to Vikramāditya. The stanza here cited is no. 529 (xiv, 43) of the drama.

[233] = Mer. 99 (Taw. 60). For the three (or even a thousand!) heads of Śiva see Hopkins, pp. 221, 222.

Then, seeing (that) read by Kālidāsa [234] in the former lacuna of the stone tablet through cleaning (it) with lac, the King rejoiced greatly.

Upon a time a new interior of (his) house (was) constructed by Bhoja for (his) pleasure. In the interior of that house a Brahmarākṣasa [235] entered even before the (formal) entry into the house and devours by night those who dwell there. Then, summoning magicians, the King endeavoured to expel him; and he, coming in, even devours the magicians and, moreover, himself keeps reciting poetry and so forth (which he has) previously learnt. The demon thus remaining right there, the King considered: 'How (can there be) escape from him?' Then said Kālidāsa: 'Sire, evidently this demon is thoroughly versed in all the text-books and (is) a good poet. So I find a way by pleasing him. Never mind the magicians; see my spell!'

So saying, he himself, going there by night, lay down. Then at the first watch the Brahmarākṣasa came, and seeing a man not (there) before, at every watch he recites a *samasyā*, an aphorism of Pāṇini.[236] Since the remainder (is) not spoken according to his mind, he kills him, thinking: 'This (is) not a Brāhman; [*72*] so he may be killed.' Thereupon observing: 'As before, this (is) a man not (here) before, so let me recite (my) *samasyā*; if he does not say the rest like it, then he may be killed,' he recites:

'"Of all, two—"'

Then said Kālidāsa:

'Causes of weal (and) woe (exist): wisdom (and) folly.'

Then (the demon) departed. Coming again at the second watch, he recites:

'"An old man with a young man—"'

Then said the poet:

'Because of (their) association is abandoned by the fair.'

The demon, coming again at the third watch, recites:

'"In a family one—"'

---

[234] Reading, with P and T, *kālidāsapaṭhitam* instead of the *kālidāsaḥ paṭhati* of V.

[235] A Brāhman who, because of sins in a former birth, becomes a demon. For formal entry into a new house cf. A. Hillebrandt, [*Indische*] *Ritualliteratur*, Strasbourg, 1897, p. 82.

[236] These aphorisms (marked by double quotation-marks in the translation) are (1) VIII, i, 1; (2) I, ii, 65; (3) IV, i, 93; (4) I, ii, 68.

Then said the poet:

'Man is pre-eminent, (he) who sustaineth the household.'

Then the demon, coming in the fourth watch, recites:

'"And a woman like a man—"'

Then said the poet:

'When she is pre-eminent, then the house (is) destroyed.' (307)

Then, recognising his own implication in the four watches, coming, delighted, at the time of dawn (and) embracing him [Kālidāsa], the demon said: 'Wise one, I am delighted; what (is) thy wish?' Kālidāsa said: 'Your Honour, leaving this house, shouldst go elsewhere.' (Saying:) 'So (be it),' he went. Straightway the King, delighted, honoured the poet greatly.

Upon a time, Bhoja, the crest-jewel of all the protectors of earth, adorning the lion-throne, a door-keeper, approaching, said: 'Sire, a poet from the Deccan-land, named Mallinātha, with (only) a remnant of a loin-cloth, is at the door.' The King said: 'Let (him) enter.' Then the poet, approaching, saying: 'Hail!' and seated at his [Bhoja's] bidding, recites:

'An elephant is beautiful with ichor, the sky with clouds, the night with the full moon, a woman with character, a horse with speed, a house with continual festivals, [73] diction with polished language, rivers with pairs of swans, a court with sages, a family with a good son, the earth with thee, the triple world with the sun.' (308)[237]

Then said the King: 'Sage, what (is) thy motive?' Then said the poet:

'(My) mother is not pleased with me nor with (her) daughter-in-law; and she neither with (my) mother nor with me; and I neither with one nor the other. Say, O King, whose fault (is) this?' (309)[238]

And the King, knowing (that to be) the fault of poverty, fulfilled the poet's wishes.

Upon a time a door-keeper, approaching, said to the King: 'Sire, a great poet named Kaviśekhara[239] is at the door.' The King said: 'Let (him) enter.' Then the poet, approaching (and) saying: 'Hail!' recites:

[237] = IS 3545; to the fourth statuette in Vikrama. SR iv, 3.

[238] Read *tuṣyati* 'is pleased' with Mer. 72 (Taw. 41), Sad. V, xlvii, 1, and IS 540 instead of the meaningless *kupyati* 'is angry' of the printed editions. In Mer. and Sad. the stanza is anonymous.

[239] According to Subhāṣ. 2455-2458, this was Amṛtadatta.

> 'O King, from the keeper of the portal have I gained ⟨rebuff⟩ ([for] I have gained an ⟨elephant⟩); from thee I desire ⟨no rebuff⟩, O Lord of Earth ([for] I desire a ⟨must-elephant⟩). (310)

Then the King, facing east, highly delighted (and) thinking (that) the whole eastern region (had been) given to the poet, faced south. Then the poet thought: 'What (is) this? The King, averting (his) face, seeth me not.' Then, coming in the southern region (and) facing (Bhoja), the poet recites:

> 'How (hath) this unprecedented skill in the bow (been) learnt by Thy Majesty? A flood of ⟨arrows⟩ cometh unto (thee; thy) ⟨bow-string⟩ goeth in another ⟨direction⟩ ([for] a flood of ⟨mendicants⟩ cometh unto [thee; thy] ⟨quality [of generosity and the like]⟩ goeth to another ⟨land⟩).' (311)[240]

Then, having mentally given the southern region also to the poet, the King faced west. The poet, going there, said:

> 'Falsely this world calleth Thy Majesty "omniscent"; one word thou knowest not (how) to say to a beggar: "(There) isn't (anything)."' (312)

Then, thinking (that) that region also (had been) given to the poet, the King faced north. The poet, approaching there also, said:

> 'Thou are wrongly said by the wise (to be) giving everything everywhere; (thy) foes have not gotten (thy) back, nor others' wives (thy) breast.' (313)[241]

Then the King, thinking (that all) his land (had been) given to the poet, arose; and the poet, not knowing his idea, again said:

> 'O King, while thou art raining everywhere with streams of gold, not (even) drops come on me, covered with an umbrella of misfortune.' (314)[242]

[74] And then the King, going to the harem, said to Queen Līlā: 'Lady, all the kingdom (hath been) given to the poet. So go with me to the forest of penance.' At that moment the sage, departing at the door, (was) asked by the aged minister[243] Buddhisāgara: 'Sage, what (hath been) given by the King?' He said: 'Nothing.' Then the minister said: 'Recite the *śloka* said there.' Then the poet recites the four *ślokas*. Then said the minister: 'Good poet, ten millions of gold are given thee; but let what is there given thee by the King be sold

[240] = Subhāṣ. 2455; ascribed to Siddhasena, addressing Vikramāditya, in Mer. 15 (Taw. 11).

[241] = IS 6923; ascribed to Siddhasena by Mer., *loc. cit.*, and Vikrama. JR (mss.) vii, 6.

[242] = IS 5738 and stanza 186, where it is spoken by an anonymous Brāhman.

[243] T, 'prime minister.'

again.' So the poet does. Then, giving ten millions of gold (and) dismissing the poet, the minister, going to the King's presence, stood (there). And then the King said to him: 'Buddhisāgara, all this kingdom (hath been) given to the poet, (and) I go with (my) wives to the forest of penance. If thy desire (be) there in the forest of penance,[244] come along with me.' Then said the minister: 'Sire, this kingdom (hath been) sold by the poet for the price of ten millions of gold, and ten millions of gold (have been) given to the sage. So the kingdom (is) Thy Majesty's. Enjoy (it)!' And then the King honoured Buddhisāgara especially.

On another occasion, wandering in a forest through love of the chase, the sun burning (his) brow, tortured in body, (and) filled with thirst, mounting (his) horse (and) desirous of water, wandering (in search of some) neighbouring (river-)bank, (but) finding it not, the King sat, utterly weary, under a great tree. Then, by chance, there met (him) a milkmaid, all (her) limbs very delicate (and) charming, desirous of selling diluted buttermilk in the city of Dhārā, and bearing a jar of diluted buttermilk. Seeing her coming (and) thinking, because of (his) thirst: 'If (only) I drink this draught in the jar of diluted buttermilk!' the King asked: 'Young (damsel), what carriest thou?' And she, thinking (it was) Bhoja by the beauty of his countenance and realising his thirst, said in metrical form, because of (her) gaze at his face:

> 'Drink, O King of Kings, (what) taketh away distress, like to the winter jasmine (and) the shell of the moon's beauty, with the savour of the perfume of the ripe wood-apple, churned by the tendril-hands of young (women).' (315)

And drinking the diluted buttermilk, the King, delighted, said to her: 'Fair-browed one, what (is) thy desire?' And, somewhat revealing (her) youth (and with her) eyes full of bewilderment, she said, mastered by rapture: 'Sire, look even upon me, a maiden.' Again she said:

> [75] 'This (my) nature of mind, best of Princes, ever longeth to see thee as the white-lotus pool the moon, the flock of *kokas* the beloved of the lotus [the sun], the host of *cātakas* the cloud, the swarm of bees the cluster of flowers, the female cuckoo the mango-tree, a wife her absent lord.' (316)[245]

The King, amazed, said: 'Very delicate one, with Queen Līlā's permission we make thee our own'; (and) conducting her to the city of Dhārā, even so he made (her) his own.

[244] I. e., to enter upon the life of a forest-hermit (see note 198).

[245] Ascribed to Rāghavacaitanya in Śārṅ. 1557. For the *koka* (*cakravāka*) see note 207; for the *cātaka*, note 137; and for the cuckoo (*kokila, pika*) note 192.

Upon a time, at the King's (ritual) bath, a golden jar, dropping from the palms of a lovely-eyed (woman) pained by Love's arrows, fell klanging on the steps. Then the King, going to the court, said to Kālidāsa: 'Good poet, fill this *samasyā*: "ṭaṭaṁṭaṭaṁṭaṁṭaṭaṭaṁṭaṭaṁṭaṁ."' Then said Kālidāsa:

'On the steps of the King's bath a golden jar, fallen from the hand of a young (woman) afflicted by love, maketh the sound ṭaṭaṁṭaṭaṁṭaṁṭaṭaṭaṁṭaṭaṁṭaṁ.' (317)

Then the King, knowing his own implication, gave (him) a lakh per syllable.

On another occasion, noble Bhoja adorning the lion-throne, a thief (was) brought to the King's presence by watchmen, and the King, seeing him, asked: "Who (is) this?' Then the watchmen said: 'Sire, property in a brothel (was) taken by this housebreaker with striking (and) felling.' Then said the King: 'This (knave) must (be) punished.' Then the thief, named Bhukkuṇḍa, said:

'Bhaṭṭi (hath) perished; Bhāravīya, in sooth, (hath) perished; Bhikṣu (hath) perished; Bhīmasena, in sooth, (hath) perished; I (am) Bhukkuṇḍa; thou, O King, (art) Lord of Earth (*bhūpati*)—the Ender [Death] (is) entered into (this) series of *bha's*!' (318)[246]

Then said the King: 'Go, Bhukkuṇḍa, go; carry off at will!'

Upon a time Bhoja, full of the chase, roving about in the forest, (but his) mind intent on rest, arriving at a pool, stayed (there) and, from weariness, slept. Then, the sun gone to the cavern of the western ocean,

There shone the night, giving happiness to the King, teeming with the blissful abundance of inconstant moonbeams. (319)

[76] Then, setting forth to the city at dawn (and) eagerly regarding the moon's orb clinging to the slope of the western mount, the King, going to the court (and) beholding the lordly poets standing in (his) presence, spoke one (verse) of a *samasyā*:

'The moon's orb clung to the slope of the western mount;'

Then said Bhavabhūti:

'The Pleiades gone in the sky because of the multitude of the sun's rays;'

---

[246] Bhaṭṭi (before 650) was the author of the *Rāvaṇavadha* or *Bhaṭṭikāvya*; Bhāravīya (also before 650) wrote the *Kirātārjunīya* (T reads *bhāraviścā 'pi*); Bhikṣu seems to be known only from a mention in Sad.; Bhīmasena was the second of the Pāṇḍu princes and a fierce and terrible hero of the *Mahābhārata*; instead of the *bhabbhāpañktāv* of P, T reads *bhabbhāvalyām*, and V *bhabhvaḥpañktāv*.

Then Daṇḍin said:

'A cool wind stirring gently, gently at dawn;'

Then said Kālidāsa:

'A host of young (women) with (their) *bimba*-lips[247] deserted by (their) lords, the moon's orb clung to the slope of the western mount.' (320)

Then the King honoured all, (but) especially did he reverence Kālidāsa.

Then upon a time, going forth from the city, with fresh water from a pool the King performed (his) skull-cleansing[248] and so forth, learnt in childhood. Through that means a young *śaphara*,[249] entering (his) skull (and) fastening itself to the great skull(-bone), did not go out. Then the King regained his city, (but) thenceforth in the King's skull (there was) pain (which), though then properly treated by the best physicians there, (was) not alleviated, the King thus (being) extremely ill night and day with a grave malady unknown to man.

(His) body, (its) happiness gone, became thin, thin like a lotus in winter time; (his) face, (its) beauty departed, as the moon's disk assailed by Rāhu's[250] mouth; his mind averse to duties to be performed as (that) of a eunuch among women; (his) sickness became more complete like fire in a dry forest. (321)

A year's space thus elapsing, his illness (was) stayed by no one whomsoever. Then, distressed in mind by swallowing divers sorts of similar medicines (and by his) malady, the noble Bhoja in some way or other addressed words with coherent sounds to Buddhisāgara standing near, plunged in an ocean of grief: 'Buddhisāgara, henceforth let no best of physicians whomsoever prolong (his) abode in our land. Go, throw all the medical textbooks of Vāgbhaṭa[251] and the rest in the river. The time of my union with the gods (is) come.' Hearing this, all the citizens and poets and the throngs in the harems had eyes (filled with) floods of dripping tears.

Then upon a time in the court of the gods the Destroyer of Strong-

[247] See note 171.

[248] A rite of Haṭhayoga (cf. R. Garbe, *Sāṃkhya und Yoga*, Strasbourg, 1896, p. 45).

[249] Cyprinus Saphore, a small fish which glistens when darting about in shallow water.

[250] See note 54.

[251] For this medical writer (at latest in the eighth century) see Winternitz, iii, 549; Jolly, *Medicin*, pp. 8-9. P reads *Bāhvaṭa*.

holds [Indra] said to the lute-ascetic [252] standing amid the host of all the ascetics: [77] 'Ascetic, what news now on earth?' Then said Nārada: 'Nothing extraordinary, Lord of the Gods. But noble King Bhoja, dwelling in the city of Dhārā, afflicted by a malady, is extremely ill; that malady of his (is) not stayed by any one whomsoever, so that even the best of physicians (are) expelled from his land by that Prince Bhoja; (and) the medical textbook itself (is) thrown away on the score that (it is) false.'

Hearing that, the Much-invoked [Indra] said this to the two Nāsatyas [253] standing near: 'Physicians of heaven, how (is) Dhanvantari's [254] textbook false?' Then they said: 'Sire, Lord of the Immortals, that textbook (is) not utterly fallacious, but this Bhoja is suffering from a malady known (only) to the immortals.' Indra: 'What (is) this unstayable malady? How (is) it known to you?' Then they said: 'Sire, skull-cleansing (was) performed by Bhoja; then a *śaphara* [255] entered; this malady (hath) that origin.' Then said Indra with smiling countenance: 'So now you must go; otherwise henceforth there would be failure of the textbook of medicine on earth. He [Bhoja], indeed, (is) the abode of Sarasvatī's sport and the upholder of textbooks.'

Then, at the bidding of the Lord of the Gods, they both, donning the raiment of Brāhmans (and) reaching the city of Dhārā, said to a door-keeper: 'Door-keeper, we (are) two physicians come from the land of Benares. Make known to noble Bhoja that, hearing that the textbook of medicine (is) deemed false by him, (we are here) for its corroboration and for the staying of his malady.' Then said the door-keeper: 'Brāhmans, the King (hath) said that no most excellent physician whosover may be admitted. The King (is) absolutely ill; this (is) not the moment for the request.' Coming out at that instant for some reason (and) seeing them, Buddhisāgara asked: 'Who (are) Your Honours?' Then they told how they (had) come. Then they (were) conducted to the King's presence by Buddhisāgara.

Then, regarding them, thinking by the beauty of (their) countenances

[252] Nārada, one of the seven sages (*ṛṣis*), inventor of the lute (*vīṇā*), and chief of the celestial musicians (*gandharvas*).

[253] The celestial twins, the Aśvins, noted for their healing powers; see Macdonell, pp. 49-54.

[254] Doubtless the medical lexicon *Dhanvantarinirghaṇṭu*, ed. Vaidyanārāyaṇa Śarma Purandhare[2], Poona, 1927; cf. Winternitz, iii, 553; Jolly, *Medicin*, p. 13. For works ascribed to Dhanvantari see Aufrecht, i, 267; ii, 57; iii, 58; for the deity himself see L. H. Gray, 'The Indian God Dhanvantari,' *Journal of the American Oriental Society*, xlii (1922), 323-337.

[255] So V; P and T, *pāṭhīnaḥ*, Silurus Pelorius or Boalis, a kind of sheat-fish.

(that they were) superhuman, (and) reflecting: 'This malady can be stayed by these,' the King honoured them greatly. Then they said: 'O King, fear not! The malady (is) gone; but thou must be somewhere alone.' Then the King did so. Then, stupefying the King with a powder of stupefaction,[256] taking (his) skull, seizing the body of the *śaphara* in a cranial sinus of it, throwing (it) into a receptacle, exactly restoring the skull by reunion, and reviving him by a resuscitant, they showed it to him. Then, seeing it, the King, astonished, asked them: 'What (is) this?' Then they said: 'O King, this (was) gotten by thee from skull-cleansing from thy youth on.' [*78*] Then the King, deeming them (to be) the Aśvins, asked (them) for the purpose of his improvement: 'What (is) wholesome for us?' Then they said:

> 'Bathing with unchilled water, milk (as) a drink, (and) the best women—this (is) wholesome for you, O mortals.'

Meanwhile the King, hearing the vocative 'O mortals' in the middle (of a line and saying:) 'If we (are) mortals, who (are) ye?' straightway grasped their hands with his hands. Then they vanished at that very instant, saying: 'The fourth quarter (of the stanza is) to be completed by Kālidāsa.' Then the King, amazed, summoning all, told the event; and all, hearing it, were astonished and amazed. Then the fourth quarter (was) completed by Kālidāsa:

> 'And bland, warm food.' (322)

Then Bhoja, deeming Kālidāsa (to be) a mortal (only) by caprice,[257] honoured (him) exceedingly. Then King Bhoja increased daily with the beauty of (his) innate strength, the Lord of Dhārā,[258] like the moon in (its) bright half.

Then upon a time, noble Bhoja adorning the lion-throne in the court adorned by the company of poet-ornaments, Kālidāsa, Bhavabhūti, Daṇḍin, Bāṇa, Mayūra, Vararuci, and the rest, a door-keeper, coming, said: 'Sire, a poet standeth at the door. Let this chit with a stanza, sent by him, be presented at (My) Lord's court.' With these words he shows it; and the King, taking it, reads:

> 'A young (woman) sending a basket to (her) lover's house by a slave-girl's hand, timidly painted a serpent, (and) above it Gaurī's beloved [Śiva], the Son of Wind [Hanuman], and a champak—the noble skilful adornment Mallinātha, lord of poets, asketh the meaning there.' (323)[259]

---

[256] *Mohacūrṇa*, very possibly opium (*mohakṛt*); see Jolly, *Medicin*, p. 30.

[257] I. e., really a god, not a man. The preceding stanza is all by the Aśvins in Sūk. cix, 119.

[258] V wisely omits 'Lord of Dhārā'; T omits 'King Bhoja.'

[259] The girl, distressed by separation from her lover, is a prey to mortal illness

Hearing this, all the assembly of sages (were) astonished. Then said Kālidāsa: 'O King, Mallinātha (is) to be summoned quickly.' Then, brought in by the door-keeper at the King's command, the poet, saying 'Hail!' to the King, (was) seated at his bidding. Then said the King to the lord of poets: 'Learned poet Mallinātha, the stanza (is) well composed.' Then Kālidāsa said: 'Why is (merely) "well" said? Thou are to be lauded for (thy) description of the conduct of the wife (of a husband) gone to another land [260] (and) by (thy) description of the contrasts between this (and) that character.' [261] Then said Bhavabhūti: 'This stanza differeth from the (conventional) description of the Son of Wind, the foe of the pleasure-grove of the Ten-Necked One [Rāvaṇa].' [262] Then a lakh of gold pieces (were) given him by the King, [79] and five elephants and ten horses (also were) given (him). Then the sage, well pleased, praises the King:

> 'O Lord Bhoja, through the water-floods of thy generosity now, I suspect, this (is) night; else how (would there be) such generosity in (regard to) visible crags, earth, (and) trees?' (324)

Then, hearing the supermundane stanza, the King again gave him three lakhs. Then the comptroller of the treasury wrote in the religious (account) book:

> 'Noble King Bhoja, hearing in the assembly a poem with a hidden pleasantry on a (woman) bereft of (her) husband, well pleased, bestoweth a lakh of gold pieces, ten excellent steeds, (and) five elephants; afterward right there, (his) mind well pleased from the excellent portrayal of (his) virtue of generosity, he gave that Mallinātha a lakh and a lakh and again a lakh.' (325)

Then upon a time King Bhoja said to Kālidāsa: 'Good poet, read us the last *śloka*.' [263] Then Kālidāsa, wroth (and) reproaching the King, straightway abandoning that land, gained the city of Ekaśilā

and implores him to avert this as Śiva swallowed the venom at the Churning of the Ocean (see note 64) and to be united with him as Śiva was with Gaurī (see note 168); she is like a dying champak with petals scattered by the wind of separation from him as the Son of Wind broke down the pleasure-grove of Rāvaṇa (cf. note 262). The stanza implies that as the woman longs for her absent darling, so the poet longs to be the recipient of Bhoja's largess.

[260] The conventional Indian type known as *proṣitā* (see Schmidt, pp. 305-307).

[261] I. e., the contrast between the cruel serpent, the great Śiva, the mighty Hanuman, and the delicate champak.

[262] A much-better known exploit of Hanuman was his destruction of Rāvaṇa's capital, Laṅkā, by means of his blazing tail, which had been greased and set on fire by the demon and his Rākṣasas.

[263] I. e., a *śloka* about Bhoja's death and also the last *śloka* of the work.

with Vilāsavatī. Then, filled with grief at separation from Kālidāsa, the King, assuming the garb of a (Śaivite) skull-bearing (ascetic), went methodically to the city of Ekaśilā to hunt for Kālidāsa. Then Kālidāsa, seeing the ascetic, asked him kindly: 'Ascetic, where (is) thy dwelling?' The ascetic says: 'Good poet, our abode (is) in the city of Dhārā.' Then said the poet: '(Is) Bhoja well there?' Then said the ascetic: 'What should I say?' Then the poet said: 'If there is extraordinary news there, tell the truth.' Then said the ascetic: 'Bhoja (is) gone to heaven.' Then the poet, falling to the ground, wails: 'Sire, without thee (there is) no abiding on earth for us, even for an instant; so I come to thy presence.' Thus wailing repeatedly, Kālidāsa made the last *śloka*:

> 'Today (hath) Dhārā no foundation,[264] Sarasvatī no support; the scholars (are) all scattered, King Bhoja gone to heaven.' (326)

When the last *śloka* (had) thus been spoken by the poet, then the ascetic fell unconscious to the ground. Then Kālidāsa, seeing him in such plight, being certain that this (was) Bhoja indeed, [*80*] (and) saying: 'Alas! alas! great King, I (have been) tricked by Thy Majesty!' straightway recited that *śloka* in another fashion:

> 'To-day (hath) Dhārā a good foundation, Sarasvatī a good support; the scholars (are) all adorned, King Bhoja gone to earth.' (327)

Then embracing him (and) doing (him) homage, Bhoja went to the city of Dhārā.[265]

[264] The word-plays *Dhārā* (the city-name), *nirādhārā*, *sadādhārā* 'without foundation, with good foundation' cannot be reproduced in English.

[265] P, but not V or T, here adds a stanza manifestly spurious and irrelevant.

POETS QUOTED IN THE BHOJAPRABANDHA

(Akālajalada [grandfather of Rājaśekhara]: *201*, Śārṅ. 777; to Cittapa, Sad. IV, xxiii, 5; to Dākṣiṇātya, Subhāṣ. 843; to Rājaśekhara, Mer. 75; anonymous in B-P.)

(Acalasiṁha: *208*, Sad. IV, lxiii, 2; to Śrīpati, V; anonymous in Sūk. xiii, 2.)

(Amṛtadatta [latter half of the fourteenth century]: *311*, Subhāṣ. 2455; to Kaviśekhara in B-P.)

(Arghaṭa: *97*, Sūk. iv, 19, and Subhāṣ. 153; to Sītā in B-P; *169*, Subhāṣ. 2277; to Vilocana's wife in B-P.)

Aśvinau: *322* (first three quarters; all to them, Sūk. cix, 119).

Kaviśekhara or Jyotirīśvara (late fifteenth century): *310-314* (*311* to Amṛtadatta, Subhāṣ. 2455; *311*, *313* to Siddhasena addressing Vikramāditya, Mer. 15; *314* = *186*, there anonymous).

Kāmadeva: *227*.

Kālidāsa (probably end of the fourth and beginning of the fifth century): *77-85* (*79* to Vallabhadeva, Sūk. iv, 18); *86* (second half; to the Paramāra Jagaddeva, Sūk. cix, 131); *88*; *112* (second half; this to Rājaśekhara, Sūk. iv, 3; all to Bhoja in the Bengali recension); *132*; *134-136*; *139*; *140* (= *51* as a commonplace); *142* (second half); *144* (to Dhanada, Vikrama. JR vii, 3); *145* (to Vyāsa, Sūk. cx, 9); *153*; *154* (second half; to Hemacandra, Mer. 147); *161* (fourth quarter-verse; all anonymous, Śārṅ. 3588); *191*; *250*; *252-253*; *258* (second half); *259*; *263* (to a group of Bhoja's poets, Śārṅ. 3717); *265* (first three lines); *274-278*; *290*; *292* (first three lines); *294* (first half); *295*; *296* (first and fourth lines); *299*; *301*; *302* (first three lines; the whole anonymous, Sad. IV, lxxxi, 2); *303* (third quarter-verse); *306* (first two lines); *307* (non-Pāṇinean portions); *317* (first three lines); *320* (third line); *322* (last quarter-verse; all to the Aśvins, Sūk. cix, 119); *326-327*.

(Kṛṣṇamiśra [second half of the eleventh century]: *270*, Sūk. cxxviii, 3; to Viśvāvasu in the Bengali recension; also in *Prabodhacandrodaya* iv, 9, and in Bhartṛhari.)

Krīḍācandra: *113-120* (*115* to Vararuci, Sad. I, xi, 5; to Candaka, Subhāṣ. 66); *123*.

(Kṣemendra [eleventh century]: *7*, Sūk. cxxv, 6; anonymous, Vikrama. SR xxi, 8; to Muñja in B-P; really from the *Pañcatantra; 29*, Sūk. cxii, 4; to Bhoja in B-P; *31*, Subhāṣ. 3152 and Sūk. cxii, 1; to Bhoja in B-P.)

Gālava (according to V 158. 7): *217* (anonymous in P and T).

Gopāla: *213-214*.

Govinda: *47-48* (*48* anonymous, Sūk. xxxi, 2); *53-56*. Govinda's father: *49-52* (*51* a commonplace repeated by Kālidāsa, *140*).

(Candaka: *115*, Subhāṣ. 66; to Vararuci, Sad. I, xi, 5; to Krīḍācandra in B-P and Śārṅ. 96.)

(Cittapa: *201*, Sad. IV, xxiii, 5; to Akālajalada, Śārṅ. 777; to Dākṣiṇātya, Subhāṣ. 843; to Rājaśekhara, Mer. 75; anonymous in B-P.)

(Jagaddeva: *86*, Sūk. cix, 131; to poetasters and Kālidāsa in B-P.)

(Jayavardhana: *209*, Subhāṣ. 2478; to Mucukunda in B-P.)

(Jayasiṁha Siddharāja [Chaulukya King of Aṇhilvāḍ, 1093-1143]: *154* [first half], Mer. 147; to Bhoja in B-P.)

Taṇḍuladeva: *164*.

(Trivikrama [early tenth century; author of the *Nalacampū* or *Damayantīkathā*?]: *5*, Vikrama. SR ix, 5; to Muñja in B-P.)

Daṇḍin (probably seventh century): *320* (second line).

(Dākṣiṇātya: *201*, Subhāṣ. 843; to Akālajalada, Śārṅ. 777, to Cittapa, Sad. IV, xxiii, 5; to Rājaśekhara, Mer. 75; anonymous in B-P.)

Dāmodara: *220*.

Devajaya (Jayadeva in the Bengali recension): *268* (to Vālmīki, Subhāṣ. 764; anonymous in Sūk. xvii, 9).

(Dhanada: *144*, Vikrama. JR vii, 3; to Kālidāsa in B-P.)

(Dhanadeva: *39*, Śārṅ. 697; to Buddhisāgara in B-P.)

(Dhanapāla [tenth century; see p. 3]: *202*, Mer. 101; to Viṣṇu in B-P; *216*, Mer. 95; to Śākalya in B-P; *288*, Mer. 102; to a poet from Jālandhara in B-P.)

Dharmadatta (only in V): *242-243*; according to the Bengali recension, to a poet from Puṣkara.

(Prahlādana [late twelfth and early thirteenth century]: *64*, Sūk. cxvi, 10; to Bhoja in P-B.)

Bāṇa (first half of the seventh century): *99-103* (*100* from the *Pañcatantra; 103* to Bhaṭṭapradyumna, Subhāṣ. 504 = Māgha, *282*); *141*; *150*; *161* (second quarter-verse; all anonymous, Śārṅ. 3588); *163; 240* in the Bengali recension; to Śāmbhavadeva, Śārṅ. 145; really from Subandhu, *Vāsavadattā* 11; Sūk. iv, 13; *244* (to Hārīta in the Bengali recension). Bāṇa's son: *247*.

Buddhisāgara (prime minster): *39-44* (*39* to Dhanadeva, Śārṅ. 697; *43* really from the *Pañcatantra*).

(Bhaṭṭapradyumna: *103* = *282*, Subhāṣ 504 [*103* to Bāṇa in B-P; *282* to Māgha in B-P and Mer. 87].)

(Bhadantajñānavarman: *226*, Sūk. xxxiii, 4; Śārṅ. 971; anonymous, Sad. IV, lvi, 5; to Maheśvara in B-P.)

(Bhartṛhari [before the middle of the seventh century]: *143*, Vikrama. SR ii, 9; JR ii, 12; to Bhoja in B-P.)

(Bhallaṭa [ninth century]: *177*, Subhāṣ. 995; to an anonymous Vaiśya in B-P.)

Bhavabhūti (first half of the eighth century): *203*, Śārṅ. 148; Sūk. iv, 29; to Bhoja in B-P; *245-246*; *248-249*; *251*; *293* (first half); *297*; *304* (first two lines); *320* (first line).

(Bhāravi [before the sixth century]: *298*, Sūk. lxvi, 8; to Vararuci in B-P.)

Bhāskara (author of the fourteenth-century [?] *Unmattarāghava*): *215* (anonymous, Sad. V, xlviii, 3).

Bhukkuṇḍa: *318*.

Bhoja (King of Dhārā, 1010-1055): *28-31* (*28* anonymous, Vikrama. SR iii, 12; *29* and *31* to Kṣemendra, Subhāṣ. 3152; Sūk. cxii, 4; cxii, 1; *38; 57-58* (*57* to Yaśovarmadeva, Sūk. cx, 48; to Vikrama, Vikrama. MR xxx, 44-45; really from the *Mahābhārata*); *61-65* (*61* to Vararuci, Subhāṣ. 473; *64* to Prahlādana, Sūk. cxvi, 10; *65* anonymous, Mer. 140); *68*; *74*; *75* (with Śaṅkara; all to Śaṅkara, Subhāṣ. 1258); *89-91* (*91* anonymous, Śārṅ. 268); *104*; *112* (first half; to Rājaśekhara, Sūk. iv, 3; all to Bhoja in the Bengali recension); *142* (first half); *143* (to Bhartṛhari, Vikrama. SR ii, 9; JR ii, 12); *154* (first half; to Jayasiṁha, Mer. 147); *158-160*; *161* (first quarter-verse; all anonymous, Śārṅ. 3588); *182* (first, third, and fifth quarter-verses); *185* (first and third quarter-verses); *189*; *198* (second and fourth quarter-verses); *200* (first three lines; the whole stanza to Vikramāditya, Subhāṣ. 3318); *203* (to Bhavabhūti, Śārṅ. 148 and Sūk. iv, 29); *236* (first half; to Harṣa, Subhāṣ. 1978); *258* (first half); *265* (first line); *291*; *292* (last line); *293* (second half); *294* (second half); *296* (first and third quarter-verses); *302* (last line; the whole anonymous, Sad. IV, lxxxi, 2); *303* (first quarter-verse); *305* (first two lines); *317* (last line); *320* (last line).

Bhoja's chowry-bearer: *212* (to a learned Brāhman girl, Mer. 71).

Bhoja's comptroller of the treasury: *190*; *196*; *211*; *219*; *228*; *231*, Śārṅ. 565; to Vikrama's treasurer, Vikrama. SR xxx, 16; JR xxx, 3; from the religious account-book, Mer. 68; to Vikramārka in B-P; *237*; *325*.

Bhoja's court-panegyrist: *230* (to Siddhasena, Mer. 15; to Haricandra, Sad. III, liv, 4).

(Bhoja's group of poets: *262*, Śārṅ. 2217; to Sītā in B-P; *263*, Śārṅ. 3717; to Kālidāsa in B-P.)

Bhoja's prime minister (named Rohaka in Mer. 64): *59-60*; *198* (first and third quarter-verses); *285-287*.

Mayūra (first half of the seventh century): *121; 193-194; 235*.

Marāla: *105*; *107*.

Mallinātha: *222* (to Vaidyabhānu, Sūk. xxxiii, 1; Śārṅ. 973); *308-309* (*308* to the fourth statuette, Vikrama. SR iv, 3; *309* anonymous, Mer. 72 and Sad. V, xlvii, 1); *323-324*.

Maheśvara: *129* (Bengali recension; to Ravigupta, Subhāṣ. 154; to Rāmeśvara in B-P); *161* (third quarter-verse; all anonymous, Śārṅ. 3588); *226* (to Bhadantajñānavarman, Sūk. xxxiii, 2; Śārṅ. 971; anonymous, Sad. IV, lvi, 5).

Māgha (second half of the seventh century): *279* (from his *Śiśupālavadha*); *281-283* (*282*, so also Mer. 87 = Bāṇa, *103*; to Bhaṭṭapradyumna, Subhāṣ. 504). Māgha's wife: *279*; *284*.

(Mātṛgupta [probably end of the fourth and beginning of the fifth century]: *232*, Subhāṣ. 3181; anonymous in B-P.)

Mucukunda: *209-210* (*209* to Jayavardhana, Subhāṣ. 2478).

Muñja (Vākpati II [974-995], younger brother of Sindhula and uncle of Bhoja): *5* (to Trivikrama, Vikrama. SR ix, 5); *7* (to Kṣemendra, Sūk. cxxv, 6; to an anonymous Brāhman, Vikrama. SR xxi, 8; really from the *Pañcatantra*); *8-17* (*11*, *13-14*, *17* also from the *Pañcatantra*; *13* to the eighteenth statuette, Vikrama. SR xviii, 5; *16* anonymous *ibid.* SR xx, 2; JR xx, 3); *27*.

(Yaśovarmadeva [King of Kanauj, eighth century]: *57*, Sūk. cx, 48; to Vikrama, Vikrama. MR xxx, 44-45; to Bhoja in B-P; really from the *Mahābhārata.*)

(Ravigupta or Bhadantaravigupta: *129*, Subhāṣ. 154; to Rāmeśvara in B-P; to Maheśvara in the Bengali recension; *133*, Subhāṣ. 244; to Sītā in B-P; *137*, Subhāṣ. 1389; to Līlāvatī in B-P.)

(Rāghavacaitanya: *316*, Śārṅ. 1557; to a milkmaid in B-P.)

(Rājaśekhara [end of the ninth and beginning of the tenth century]: *112*, Sūk. iv, 3; to Bhoja and Kālidāsa in B-P; *201*, Mer. 75; to Akālajalada, Śārṅ. 777; to Cittapa, Sad. IV, xxiii, 5; to Dākṣiṇātya, Subhāṣ. 843; anonymous in B-P.)

(Rājendra: *130* in the Bengali recension; to Rāmeśvara in B-P.)

Rāmeśvara: *124-130* (*129* to Ravigupta, Subhāṣ. 154; to Maheśvara in the Bengali recension; *130* to Rājendra in the Bengali recension).

Lakṣmīdhara: *92-93*.

Līlā(vatī) (Chief Queen of Bhoja): *137-138* (*137* to Ravigupta, Subhāṣ. 1389); *147-149* (*148* from the *Hitopadeśa*; anonymous, Sūk. cxx, 8).

Vatsarāja (tenth century): *18-26.* Vatsarāja's brother: *32-37.*

Vararuci: *61,* Subhāṣ. *473*; to Bhoja in B-P; *115,* Sad. I, xi, 5; to Krīḍācandra in B-P and Śārṅ. 96; to Candaka, Subhāṣ 66; *122-123* (*122* to Harihara, Sūk. iv, 35); *298* (to Bhāravi, Sūk. lxvi, 8).

(Vallabhadeva: *79,* Sūk. iv, 18; to Kālidāsa in B-P.)

(Vālmīki [author of the *Rāmāyaṇa*]: *268,* Subhāṣ. 764; anonymous, Sūk. xvii, 9; to Devajaya in B-P.)

Vāsudeva: *197.*

Vikramārka, Vikramāditya, or Vikrama (Candragupta II, *c.* 375-413): *57,* Vikrama. MR xxx, 44-45; to Yaśovarmadeva, Sūk. cx, 48; to Bhoja in B-P; really from the *Mahābhārata*; *200,* Subhāṣ. 3318; to Bhoja and Somanātha's thief in B-P; *229*; *231,* to Bhoja's comptroller of the treasury, Śārṅ. 565; to Vikrama's treasurer, Vikrama. SR xxx, 16; JR xxx, 3; from Vikrama's religious account-book, Mer. 68; *313,* Vikrama. JR (mss.) vii, 6; to Siddhasena, Mer. 15; to Kavi-śekhara in B-P.

Vilāsavatī (Kālidāsa's mistress): *146*; *155* (anonymous, Sūk. cx, 42); *156* (anonymous, Śārṅ. 1438); *157.* Vilāsavatī's maid: *152.*

Vilocana and family: *167-171* (*169* to Arghaṭa, Subhāṣ. 2277; *170* anonymous, Vikrama. JR III, a, 3).

Viśvāvasu: *270,* in the Bengali recension only (from the eleventh-century *Prabodhacandrodaya* of Kṛṣṇamiśra, iv, 19).

(Viśveśvara: *204,* Sad. IV, lxii, 5; to Viṣṇu in B-P.)

Viṣṇu: *202*; to Dhanapāla, Mer. 101; *204*; to Viśveśvara, Sad. IV, lxii, 5; *205.*

(Vaidyabhānu: *222,* Sūk. xxxi, 1; Śārṅ. 973; to Mallinātha in B-P.)

(Vyāsa [putative author of the *Mahābhārata* and arranger of the Vedas and Purāṇas]: *145,* Sūk. cx, 9; to Kālidāsa in B-P.)

Śakunta: *106*; *108-110.*

Śaṅkara: *75* (with Bhoja; all to Śaṅkara, Subhāṣ. 1258); *76*; *241,* Śārṅ. 1529; anonymous in B-P.

Śākalya: *216*; to Dhanapāla, Mer. 95.

Śāmbhavadeva: *239-240* (*240* really from Subandhu, *Vāsavadattā* 11; Sūk. iv, 13; to Bāṇa in the Bengali recension; to Śāmbhavadeva, Śārṅ. 145).

Śivaśarman: *300.*

Śukadeva: *195.*

Śrīpati: *208* (only V; to Acalasiṁha, Sad. IV, lxiii, 2; anonymous, Sūk. xiii, 2).

(Śrutadhara: *67, 69,* Sūk. xxxii, 4-5; to a Kaliṅga poet in B-P.)

(Sarasvatīkuṭumba's daughter: *289,* Śārṅ. 511; to Sītā in B-P.)

(Siddhasena: *230,* Mer. 15; to Haricandra, Sad. IV, liv, 4; to Bhoja's court-panegyrist in B-P; *311-313,* Mer. 15; to Kaviśekhara in B-P; *313* to Vikrama, Vikrama. JR [mss.] vii, 6.)

Sindhula (King of Dhārā, *c.* 995-1010, and father of Bhoja): *1-3.*

Sītā (cf. R. Pischel, 'Die Dichterin Çîtâ,' *Festgruss an Otto von Böhtlingk*, Stuttgart, 1888, pp. 92-94): *97* (to Arghaṭa, Sūk. iv, 19, and Subhās. 153); *131; 133* (to Ravigupta, Subhāṣ. 244); *192*; *262* (to Bhoja's group of poets, Śārṅ. 2217); *289* (to Sarasvatīkuṭumba's daughter, Śārṅ. 511).

Sīmanta: *172-173*; *207* = Bhartṛhari i, 35.

(Subandhu [somewhat after 606]: *240* = *Vāsavadattā* 11; Sūk. iv, 13; to Śāmbhavadeva in B-P and Śārṅ. 145; to Bāṇa in the Bengali recension.)

Somanātha: *206.* Somanātha's thief: *199*; *200* (fourth line; all to Vikramāditya, Subhāṣ. 3318).

(Haricandra: *230,* Sad. III, liv, 4; to Siddhasena, Mer. 15; to Bhoja's court-panegyrist in B-P.)

Hariśarman: *269.*

(Harihara: *122,* Sūk. iv, 35; to Vararuci in B-P.)

(Harṣa [King of Thāṇeśar and Kanauj, *c.* 606-648]: *236* [first half], Subhāṣ. 1978; to Bhoja in B-P.)

(Hārīta: *244* in the Bengali recension; to Bāṇa in B-P.)

(Hemacandra [twelfth century]: *154* [second half], Mer. 147; to Kālidāsa in B-P.)

Stanzas Ascribed to Unspecified Poets

Anonymous: *4; 7,* Vikrama. SR xxi, 8; to Kṣemendra, Sūk. cxxv, 3; to Muñja in B-P; really from the *Pañcatantra; 16,* Vikrama. SR xx, 2; JR xx, 3; to Muñja in B-P; *28,* Vikrama. SR iii, 12; to Bhoja in B-P; *45-46, 64,* Mer. 140; to Bhoja in B-P; *48*: Sūk. xxxi, 2; to Govinda in B-P; *72-73*; *86* (first line; all to the Paramāra Jagaddeva, Sūk. cix, 131); *91*: Śārṅ. 268; to Bhoja in B-P; *136; 148*: Sūk. cxx, 8; to Līlāvatī in B-P; *151; 155-156,* Sūk. cx, 42; Śārṅ. 1438; to Vilāsavatī in B-P; *161,* Śārṅ. 3588; to Bhoja, Bāṇa, Maheśvara, and Kālidāsa in B-P; *162; 165-166; 170,* Vikrama. JR III, a, 3; to Vilocana's son in B-P; *174; 181; 183-184; 185* (second and fourth quarter-verses; *186* (= *314,* there spoken by Kaviśekhara); *187-188; 201* B-P; to Akālajalada, Śārṅ. 777; to Cittapa, Sad. IV, xxiii, 5; to Dākṣiṇātya, Subhāṣ. 843; to Rājaśekhara, Mer. 15; *208*: Sūk. xiii, 2; to Acalasiṁha, Sad. IV, lxiii, 2; to Śrīpati in V; *212,* Mer. 71; to Bhoja's chowry-bearer in B-P; *215,* Sad. V, xlviii, 3; to Bhāskara in B-P; *218,* B-P, from Bilhaṇa's eleventh-century *Vikramāṅkadevacarita* ix, 113; *223-225; 226,* Sad. IV, lvi, 5; to Bhadantajñānavarman, Sūk. xxxiii, 4, and Śārṅ. 971; to Maheśvara in B-P; *232-234* (*232* to Mātṛgupta, Subhāṣ. 3181); *238; 241* to Śaṅkara, Śārṅ. 1529; *254-255; 266-267; 268,* Sūk. xvii, 9; to Vālmīki, Subhāṣ. 764; to Devajaya in B-P; *270-273* (*270* to Kṛṣṇamiśra, Sūk. cxxviii, 3, and in his *Prabodhacandrodaya* iv, 9; also in Bhartṛhari); *280; 302,* Sad. II, lxxxi, 2; to Bhoja and Kālidāsa in B-P; *309,* Mer. 72 and Sad. V, xlvii, 1; to Mallinātha in B-P; *319; 321.*

Astrologer: *4*; *6.*

Brahmarākṣasa: *307* (quotations from Pāṇini).

Door-keepers: *87.*

Father: *111.*

Garland-maker's wife: *264.*

Hunter's wife: *182* (second and fourth quarters of the first verse and last three quarters of the second).

Lute-poet: *260.*

Milkmaid: *315-316* (*316* to Rāghavacaitanya, Śārṅ. 1557).

Poet from Jālandhara: *288*: to Dhanapāla, Mer. 102; from Kaliṅga: *66-67, 69-71* (*67, 69* to Śrutadhara, Sūk. xxxii, 4-5); from Kāśmīr: *257*; from Konkan: *256*; from Puṣkara: *242-243* in the Bengali recension; to Dharmadatta in V.

Potter and his wife: *175-176.*

Slave-girl: *225.*

Sorcerer: *223-224.*

Stage-manager's wife: *221.*

Statuettes: *13,* eighteenth, Vikrama. SR xviii, 5; to Muñja in B-P; *308,* fourth, Vikrama. iv, 3; to Mallinātha in B-P.

Thieves: *199*; *200* (fourth verse); *236* (second half).

Vaiśya: *177-180* (*177* to Bhallaṭa, Subhāṣ. 995).

Weaver: *94-96*; *98.*

Yogi: *45-46.*

METRES (EXCEPT ŚLOKAS) OF THE BHOJAPRABANDHA

A. *Samavṛttas* (stanzas having the same number of syllables in each line).

a. Eleven syllables per line.

i. Svāgatā: – ⏑ – ⏑ ⏑ ⏑ – ⏑ ⏑ – –: 56, 324.
ii. Rathoddhatā: – ⏑ – ⏑ ⏑ ⏑ – ⏑ – ⏑ –: 188, 288.
iii. Śālinī: – – – –|– ⏑ – – ⏑ – – (4 + 7): 318.
iv. Indravajrā: – – ⏑ – – ⏑ ⏑ – ⏑ – –: 153.
v. Upendravajrā: ⏑ – ⏑ – – ⏑ ⏑ – ⏑ – –: 155, 163.
vi. Upajāti: various combinations of Indravajrā and Upendravajrā: 40, 81, 90, 92, 98, 101, 119, 135, 143, 218, 277, 278, 317.

b. Twelve syllables per line.

i. Vaṁśasthā: ⏑ – ⏑ – – ⏑ ⏑ – ⏑ – ⏑ –: 58, 76, 292, 299.
ii. Drutavilambita: ⏑ ⏑ ⏑ – ⏑ ⏑ – ⏑ ⏑ – ⏑ –: 181, 206.
iii. Toṭaka: ⏑ ⏑ – ⏑ ⏑ – ⏑ ⏑ – ⏑ ⏑ –: 297, 315.

c. Thirteen syllables per line.

i. Praharṣiṇī: – – –|⏑ ⏑ ⏑ ⏑ – ⏑ – ⏑ – – (3 + 10): 298.

d. Fourteen syllables per line.

i. Vasantatilakā: – – ⏑ – ⏑ ⏑ ⏑ – ⏑ ⏑ – ⏑ – –: 5, 7, 94, 138, 177, 200, 204, 216, 225, 235, 280-281.

e. Fifteen syllables per line.

i. Mālinī: ⏑ ⏑ ⏑ ⏑ ⏑ ⏑ – –|– ⏑ – – ⏑ – – (8 + 7): 24, 77, 113, 208, 265, 279, 320.

f. Seventeen syllables per line.

i. Śikhariṇī: ⏑ – – – – –|⏑ ⏑ ⏑ ⏑ ⏑ – – ⏑ ⏑ ⏑ – (6 + 11): 82, 96, 115, 122, 168-171, 183, 236-238, 244, 248, 252, 263, 270.
ii. Hariṇī: ⏑ ⏑ ⏑ ⏑ ⏑ –|– – – –|⏑ – ⏑ ⏑ – ⏑ – (6 + 4 + 7): 207, 262.
iii. Mandākrāntā: – – – –|⏑ ⏑ ⏑ ⏑ ⏑ –|– ⏑ – – ⏑ – – (4 + 6 + 7): 245, 307, 323.
iv. Pṛthvī: ⏑ – ⏑ ⏑ ⏑ – ⏑ –|⏑ ⏑ ⏑ – ⏑ – – ⏑ – (8 + 9): 264, 267.

g. Nineteen syllables per line.

i. Śārdūlavikrīḍita: – – – ⏑ ⏑ – ⏑ – ⏑ ⏑ ⏑ –|– – ⏑ – – ⏑ – (12 + 7): 28-29, 31, 38, 75, 84, 95, 172, 182, 197, 201-202, 212, 214-215, 217, 220, 226, 229, 231-232, 239, 241, 246, 251-252, 255, 257-258, 260-261, 266, 268, 273, 275, 302, 308, 316, 321.

h. Twenty-one syllables per line.

i. Sragdharā: – – – – ⏑ – –|⏑ ⏑ ⏑ ⏑ ⏑ ⏑ –|– ⏑ – – ⏑ – – (7 + 7 + 7): 83, 85, 227, 230, 243, 259, 276, 325.

B. *Ardhasamavṛttas* (stanzas having a different number of syllables in each line).

a. Eleven syllables in the first line, twelve in the second.

i. Vasantamālikā: ⏑⏑–⏑⏑–⏑–⏑––‖⏑⏑––⏑⏑–⏑–⏑––: 293-294.

b. Twelve syllables in the first line, thirteen in the second.

i. Puṣpitāgrā: ⏑⏑⏑⏑⏑⏑–⏑–⏑––‖⏑⏑⏑⏑–⏑⏑–⏑–⏑––: 161, 304-306.

C. *Jātis* (stanzas measured by *mātrās* [syllabic instances, *morae*], a long *mātrā* equal to two short ones).

i. Āryā: twelve *mātrās* in the first and third quarters, eighteen in the second, and fifteen in the fourth, i. e., 12 + 18 = 30; 12 + 15 = 27; 57 in all: 25, 39, 49, 51 (= 140), 67, 73, 78, 88, 97, 99, 102, 111, 116-117, 129, 133-134, 137, 144, 147, 222, 240, 285, 301, 309.

ii. Gīti: twelve *mātrās* in the first and third quarters, eighteen in the second and fourth, i. e., 12 + 18 = 30; 12 + 18 = 30; 60 in all: 26, 30, 45, 69, 79, 154, 174, 178, 290-291.

iii. Mātrāsamaka: sixteen *mātrās* in each quarter; 64 in all: 8-9.

LEXICOGRAPHICAL ADDITIONS

(* prefixed to a word or meaning indicates that such word or meaning is cited in Otto von Böhtlingk's *Sanskrit-Wörterbuch in kürzerer Fassung*, 7 parts, Petrograd, 1879-89, or in Richard Schmidt's *Nachträge zum Sanskrit-Wörterbuch in kürzerer Fassung von Otto Böhtlingk*, Leipzig, 1928, only on the authority of native lexicographers.

° prefixed to a word or meaning indicates that such word or meaning is entirely omitted by von Böhtlingk and Schmidt.

The references are to page and line of P.)

akṣara- (recorded by M. Monier-Williams, *Sanskrit-English Dictionary*, new ed., Oxford, 1899, 3[b]; 70. 3, 7) : °letter.

akhedam (adverb; 60. 28) : °unwearyingly.

**adhobhūmi-* (52. 23) : ground-floor.

°*anavadhāraṇa-* (70. 1) : lack of ascertainment, indecision.

°*anādṛtya* (gerund; recorded by Monier-Williams, 28[a]; 45. 12) : without respecting, despising, regardless of.

°*anudyamin-* (58. 28) : not striving, not exerting oneself.

°*antepura-* (4. 4) : Royal palace, gynaeceum.

**andha-* (27. 24) : water.

°*apadhvani-* (27. 13) : unpleasant sound.

apara- (15. 10) : °not different from.

°*aparādhitva-* (recorded by Monier-Williams, 51[a]; 28. 5) : guilt.

°*apātavant-* (10. 28) : not having a fall.

°*apāṁnidhi-* (recorded by Monier-Williams, 47[c] as *; 6. 23) : ocean.

°*abjavat* (adverb; 76. 19) : like a lotus.

°*abhauma-* (16. 18) : non-earthly (i. e., celestial).

°*ayacchant-* (12. 12) : not withholding.

arc- + *samabhi* (14. 29) : °adorn.

avaśeṣam (adverb; 45. 10) : °except.

°*avācyam* (adverb; 29. 23) : unspeakably.

°*avāraṇa-* (73. 11) : absence of rebuff.

asaṅgati- (50. 16) : °disunion.

°*ākumbha-* (44. 13) : up to the frontal lobe (of an elephant).

°*ānuṣaṅgin-* (65. 23) : inherent, concomitant.

°*ānetukāma-* (16. 29) : desiring to fetch.

°*ābhūṣaṇa-* (55. 24) : ornament.

°*āmalakavat* (adverb; 9. 10; 50. 11; 70. 6-7) : like a myrobalan.

āyatākṣī (71. 3) : °Sītā (long-eyed).

°*ārtivat* (adverb; 51. 10) : like the distress.

°*āliṅganavat* (adverb; 51. 11) : like an embrace.

°*ekākitā-* (T *ekākin-*; 37. 20) : oneness, loneliness.

°*kacatas* (adverb; 66. 3) : from the hair of the head.

°*kaṇṭhastha-* (recorded by Monier-Williams, 245[c]; 1. 22) : on the tip of one's tongue (lit., standing in the throat).

kaniṣṭha- (7. 19) : *younger brother.

**kandalī-* (59. 14) : banner.

**kamaṇḍalu-* (recorded by Monier-Williams, 252b; 34. 22) : hermit's water-pot.
°*karotikāpuṭa-* (77. 26) : cranial sinus.
kalāvid- (26. 26) : °finding the digits (of the moon).
°*kalpadrumay-* (45. 15) : give the illusion of the wishing-tree.
°*kāryajāta-* (4. 22) : aggregate of activities.
kālidāsa- (26. 26) : °servant of the dark cloud-mass, or, servant of night (cf. *kālikā-* dark cloud-mass and *kālī-* *night).
°*kiṁcidvidyā-* (30. 16) : some (small) knowledge.
°*kumbhilaka-* (75. 18) : housebreaker.
kula- (77. 27) : *body.
kulanāśa- (30. 21) : °destruction of race.
°*kulīnatā-* (recorded by Monier-Williams, 295c; 12. 28) : family rank.
kṛtyaśeṣa- (64. 18) : °what remains to be done.
°*kośādhikārin-* (40. 26) : comptroller of the treasury.
°*kautūhalin-* (41. 4; 44. 17; also in *Kādambarī*, A. A. M. Scharpé, *Bāṇa's Kādambarī*, Louvain [1937], 463) : curious about, deeply interested in, eager for.
krīḍācandra- (23. 2) : °play-moon.
°*krīḍīkar-* (48. 6) : make sport, jest.
°*kroṅkāra-* (42. 2) : making (the sound) *kron* (of crows).
°*gad- + sam* (57. 29) : call, name.
gandha- (54. 13) : *connexion, relation (of verse with verse).
gam- + antar (46. 23) : °go into (the harem).
gaurīkānta- (78. 21) : °beloved of Gaurī (epithet of Śiva).
ghaṭā- (56. 22) : °balance.
°*ghargharī-* (47. 29) : rattling, rattle.
°*cañcaladṛś-* (37. 2) : possessing a fleeting glance (woman).
cañcū- (60. 14) : °mouth (contemptuously; lit., beak).
°*caramagrantha-* (79. 14) : last *śloka* (i. e., on death and also of a book).
°*cāturyavant-* (1. 19) : possessed of skill.
°*cittavat* (adverb; 51. 10) : like thought.
°*chāyamukha-* (50. 20) : having the face in the shade.
°*janatas* (adverb; 50. 24) : from people.
°*jalavat* (adverb; 51. 27) : like water.
jālaka- (P and T; V *jāluka-*, recorded by Schmidt, 191c; 70. 21) : °fisherman.
°*tadarthin-* (12. 7) : desiring that.
°*tapanakara-* (39. 22) : heat-maker (i. e., sun).
tarala- (43. 28) : °spirited (of horses).
°*taruṇīkṛta-* (24. 29) : made young.
tulā- (51. 20) : °weighing of one's self against gold or other valuable substance (Hindī *tulā*).
°*tuṣārācala-* (44. 20) : snow-mountain, Himālaya.
°*tṛṇakaṇay-* (47. 3) : become a blade of grass.
°*tritaya-* (41. 29) : third.
**tviṣāmpati-* (37. 16) : sun.
daśana- (53. 5) : °tusk (of an elephant).
**dālī-* (27. 20, 22) : broth.
°*dāsavat* (adverb; 57. 4; 64. 14) : like a slave.
°*duḥkhabhāga-* (11. 20) : unhappy, unfortunate.
°*durghaṭīkar-* (28. 11) : make hard to join.
dharmapattra- (41. 19; 53. 2; 79. 8) : °record-book of disbursements for pious purposes (= °*puṇyapattra-* 42. 25; 51. 7-8).

**dhārādhara-* (50. 14) : sword.

dhaureya- (recorded by Monier-Williams, 520c, as *; 43. 4) : °fit to bear a burden.

°*dhvanidoṣa-* (71. 7) : cacophony, discord.

naṭ- + *ud* (60. 17) : °make a show, pretence, of.

**nāgādhipa-* (54. 3) : serpent-lord (i. e., Vāsuki).

°*nālīkajanman-* (16. 20) : whose birth is from the lotus.

°*niranuja-* (60. 6) : without a younger brother.

°*nirapatyaka-* (60. 6) : without children, childless.

°*nirbāndhava-* (60. 5) : without kinsfolk.

°*nirhāṭaka-* (60. 6) : without gold, penniless.

°*nistrapatva-* (41. 13) : shamelessness.

°*niḥsuhṛd-* (60. 5) : without friends, friendless.

°*niḥstrīka-* (60. 6) : without a wife.

°*pakṣagraha-* (60. 15) : (1) possession of a wing; (2) partisanship, taking of sides.

°*paṅktikaṇṭha-* (78. 29) : having ten necks (epithet of Rāvaṇa).

pathya- (27. 18, 19) : °medicine (for the meaning 'diet' see Schmidt, 244a).

pada- (20. 23) : *protection.

padajña- (33. 7) : °foot-knower, tracker (of criminals).

°*padajñāna-* (33. 4) : foot-knowledge, skill in tracking (criminals).

padapaddhati- (59. 15) : °sequence of words.

°*parahṛdaya-* (67. 22) : very secret, deep secret.

paruṣa- (20. 5) : °hardness.

pallava- (cf. Schmidt, 250c; 54. 12) : *strength.

pātaka- (cf. Monier-Williams, 616c; 10. 19) : °cause of downfall, evil.

°*pāramparya-* (4. 9) : successor.

pāśaka- (5. 7) : °basest of (lit., trap, snare).

pitṛkalpa- (47. 24) : °almost the same as a father, like a father.

°*puṇyapattra-* (42. 25; 51. 7-8) : record-book of disbursements for pious purposes (= *dharmapattra-*, 41. 19; 53. 2; 79. 8).

paulastya- (recorded by Monier-Williams, 652a; 36. 23) : °Rāvaṇa.

°*pracchannaveṣa-* (19. 29; 67. 24) : disguised.

°*pratipattra-* (13. 5) : leaf by leaf, every leaf.

°*pratipārthiva-* (50. 17) : hostile Prince or King.

pratibhaṭa- (78. 28) : °equation.

°*pratibhāmbhas-* (22. 11) : mind-water (synonym of Lake Mānasa).

°*pratiyāmam* (adverb; 71. 29) : at every watch (of four hours of the night).

°*pratyupāyam* (adverb; 27. 1) : stratagem by stratagem, craftily.

°*prathamarātri-* (47. 17) : beginning of night.

°*prapañcacatura-* (51. 22) : manifoldly skilled.

prapada- (54. 12) : °exalted verse.

°*bahulapakṣaśaśin-* (64. 23) : dark half of the moon.

**bhavādṛś-* (recorded by Monier-Williams, 749c; 65. 23) : one like Thine Honour.

bhitti- (38. 28) : *region, area.

°*bhiṣakśāstra-* (77. 12) : text-book of medicine.

bhukta- (29. 8) : ° (sexual) enjoyment.

°*bhūmbhārava-* (35. 25, 26) : cry of *bhūmbhā*.

°*bheṣajakośa-* (76. 27) : text-book of medicine.

°*bhogārha-* (recorded by Monier-Williams, 767c; 69. 24) : worth enjoying.

**maḍḍaka-* (cf. **maḍḍuka-*, **maṇḍuka-*, recorded by T. Zachariae, *Beiträge zur indischen Lexicographie*, Berlin, 1883, 72, and Monier-Williams, 774[b]; 5. 29) : sort of drum.

°*maṇḍalendra-* (24. 26) : sovereign, lord of a district.

madhupa- (12. 26) : °drunkard (recorded by Monier-Williams, 780[a]).

madhura- (55. 1) : *sweetness.

°*mukhyāmātya-* (1. 4, 16) : chief minister, prime minister.

mud- + *pra* (30. 28) : °set (of the moon).

°*mṛgavairin-* (38. 29) : foe of beasts, lion.

°*mohabhara-* (V °*mohatara-*; 19. 24) : burden of folly.

yajñeśvara- (66. 9, 11) : Lord of Sacrifice, °Agni, °fire.

yamin- (61. 24) : °concentrating upon.

°*yugalīya-* (66. 2, 3) : pair.

°*riktaśākhin-* (35. 18) : devoid of Vedic recension (better the Bengali recension, °*jāḍyaśākhin-* tree of stupidity).

rukma- (32. 15) : °gold piece.

**ruṭ-* (60. 12) : caw, crow.

rudrakalpa- (9. 14) : °like Rudra.

°*lāghavakara-* (64. 4) : degrading.

°*lī-* + *vyā* (55. 26) : hide, vanish.

°*līlāmānuṣa-* (78. 12) : man for mere caprice, only apparently a man.

°*vakritagrīva-* (10. 21 = 26. 16) : having the neck bent (away from), averse to.

°*vajravat* (adverb; 7. 15) : like a thunderbolt.

**vadhū-* (57. 14) : daughter-in-law.

°*vanyakarin-* (44. 13) : wild elephant.

var + *vyā* (47. 8) : °cover, hide, conceal (cf. Monier-Williams, 1039[a]).

vallabha- (27. 24) : *supervisor.

°*vāḍabatā-* (42. 21) : state of being a mare.

°*vikāsika-* (V °*vikāśika-*; 57. 24) : brilliance.

°*vikrītukāma-* (V and T °*vikretukāma-*; 74. 18) : desirous of selling.

vicāra- (62. 10) : °a wandering, roving.

°*vibhūpāla-* (14. 24) : without a King.

vilakṣaṇa- (13. 2) : °abashed, embarrassed.

°*visphālana-* (67. 27) : clapping of hands.

°*vīṇāmuni-* (76. 30) : lute-poet (epithet of Nārada).

°*veśyālampaṭā-* (62. 14) : lust for courtesans.

°*śayanabhavana-* (43. 7) : bed-chamber.

°*śodhanatas* (adverb; 77. 30) : from cleansing.

°*saṁśodhanīya-* (V, T *śodhanīya-*; 56. 16) : to be completely cleansed, investigated, tested.

°*sañjīvinī-* (77. 28) : analeptic.

°*sadādhāra-* (80. 3) : having good foundation.

°*sadālamba-* (80. 3) : having good support.

°*sandhānakaraṇī-* (77. 27) : reunion.

°*sapādaśata-* (35. 6) : one hundred with a quarter, 125.

°*samabhyarcita-* (14. 29) : adorned.

°*sambhāragṛha-* (20. 27, 29) : store-house.

sarasa- (60. 10) : °zeal, eagerness, longing.

°*sarasiruh-* (34. 15) : lotus (lit., growing in a lake).

°*sahāyārtha-* (7. 6) : for the sake of companionship (cf. Monier-Williams, 1195[a]).

sāhasāñka- (19. 2) : °characterised by daring (cf. Monier-Williams, 1212[b]).
sunaya- (10. 17) : *shrewd.
°*suparicaya-* (V °*svaparicaya-*; 47. 24) : good acquaintance, good knowledge.
sumati- (72. 6) : °wisdom.
suvarṇa- (53. 1, 5; 79. 1) : °gold piece (recorded by Monier-Williams, 1236[b]).
°*susmita-* (56. 3) : sweet smile.
°*spardhālu-* (55. 13; 60. 19) : rivalling, rival.
°*svavadha-* (64. 4) : self-killing, suicide.
svastha- (7. 13) : °independent, self-sufficient (cf. Monier-Williams, 1277[c]).
°*svāduvid-* (18. 2) : knowing taste or flavour.
°*haṭhatas* (adverb; 19. 10) : violently, by force.
hāṭaka- (51. 20) : °gold piece, gold coin.
°*humbhāva-* (5. 25) : uproar.